Virginia M. Crawford

Studies in Foreign Literature

Crawford, Virginia M.

Studies in Foreign Literature

ISBN/EAN: 978-3-86741-427-2
First published in 2010 by Europaeischer Hochschulverlag GmbH & Co KG, Bremen, Germany.

© Europaeischer Hochschulverlag GmbH & Co KG, Fahrenheitstr. 1, D-28359 Bremen (www.ehv-online.com). All rights reserved.

This book is a reproduction of an out of print title and has originally been published by Duckworth & Co, London (1899). Because no electronic master copies of this title could be obtained, the publisher had to reuse old copies of the text. We therefore apologize for any possible loss in quality.

STUDIES IN
FOREIGN LITERATURE

BY

VIRGINIA M. CRAWFORD

LONDON
DUCKWORTH & CO
3 HENRIETTA STREET COVENT GARDEN

THE essays on Verhaeren and on Maeterlinck appeared in their original form in the *Fortnightly Review*, and are reprinted here, after considerable revision, with the kind consent of the editor. My thanks are also due to the editor of *Cosmopolis* for permission to reproduce the essay on D'Annunzio, and to the editors of the *Contemporary Review* and the *Month* for allowing me to republish the essays respectively on Daudet and on Sienkiewicz.

CONTENTS

	PAGE
THE PRESENT DECADENCE IN FRANCE	1
CYRANO DE BERGERAC	27
ALPHONSE DAUDET	49
J. K. HUYSMANS	78
EMILE VERHAEREN	106
MAURICE MAETERLINCK	139
A SINGER OF BRUGES	175
GABRIELE D'ANNUNZIO	186
ANTONIO FOGAZZARO	219
HENRYK SIENKIEWICZ	248
WAR AND PEACE	276

THE PRESENT DECADENCE IN FRANCE

It is impossible not to believe in the existence of some absolute standard of taste, some unerring criterion by which the good and the bad in art may be appraised. For the critic, as for the theologian, some dogmatic basis which it were impious to undermine would appear to be a necessity. Yet when we seek for the evidence of such a standard in practical criticism, it would seem to be nonexistent. I know of nothing so arbitrary and illogical as the criticisms on art and literature which appear in the daily papers, save only the still wilder freaks perpetrated by untrammelled public opinion. Who can explain why Marie Corelli, whom even the critics are agreed in accepting as the type of all that is unliterary and meretricious, should command a larger sale for her novels than any living English writer?

Surely no one will venture to assert that circulation is a test of literary achievement? *Jude the Obscure* obtained a wider publicity than any of its predecessors, yet it was unmistakably the worst book that Mr. Hardy has ever written. Mrs. Humphry Ward, we know, was approved by Mr. Gladstone, and the critics are never weary of dwelling on her serious and painstaking qualities, on her unimpeachable morality. Yet Mrs. Ward is no more an artist than is Marie Corelli, and the popularity enjoyed by both goes to prove the undiscerning quality of public admiration when we remember that contemporaneously it has cost George Meredith nearly half a century of labour to achieve a general reputation at all. The public may not have discovered it, but none the less *Richard Feverel* is one of the few beautiful novels in the English language.

It is this unreasonableness of public opinion in matters of art that has led some critics to declare in their haste that—as far at least as the English nation is concerned—art must be bad if it is to be popular. But the problem cannot fairly be disposed of in this summary fashion.

Else why is it that no painter of recent years has been more popular than Millais, indisputably one of the greatest of all our English painters? Why is it that no play is so certain of a prolonged success as a great Shakespeare revival? There is a continual and growing demand for the very best music, and a Beethoven symphony to-day will attract as large an audience as a ballad concert. These assuredly are reliable tests of a cultivated artistic sense. Yet, once again, when we bear in mind that the same public has never accorded the rightful measure of recognition to Swinburne, or to Coventry Patmore, or to John Keats; and when we remember further that Rudyard Kipling, alone of living poets, has been able to realise a fortune by his verse, we are ready to turn aside in despair from so baffling a controversy.

Were I tempted to generalise on this subject, I would say that no one who receives instantaneous recognition in England is ever deserving of lasting fame. It is our intuitions that are at fault; our deliberate judgments are less liable to ross error. It is only what is superficial and commonplace and obvious—something that corresponds to the familiar emotions of the average mind—that rivets the immediate attention of the multitude. A great work of art—even for those most susceptible to its influence—creeps gradually into our life, endearing itself by degrees to our inmost consciousness, ever revealing fresh secrets of truth and beauty. Even where our ultimate discernment is to be relied on, our immediate impressions may be quite untrustworthy. The supreme test of a book is not whether we sit up half the night to finish it, but whether we turn to it again and again. It stands therefore to reason that the reviews of books published on the day of issue are, for the most part, entirely valueless. They are the outcome of hasty writing and undigested reading, and they tend to build up a body of false opinion whose destruction must be left to the slow processes of time. Sometimes it happens that we neglect our men of genius until long after their death; at other times we awake to a consciousness of their influence on life just when that influence is becoming a thing of the past. Our chronology is at fault, and we worship genius in writers in their decadence just as we applaud singers past their prime. When Ibsen wrote *Ghosts* and *The Doll's House*, and that most symbolical of all his plays, *The Wild Duck*, the English public knew nothing of him. Fashion had not turned in the direction of Norwegian drama. To-day we welcome with reverential awe the gloomy incoherent productions of his embittered old age. It is something of the same kind that we are doing in reference to contemporary French literature. Slowly we have come to realise that in the middle of the present century there was a grandeur of conception and a power of execution among imaginative French writers which our English novelists have never been able to equal. And the admiration which was due then, we lavish to-day. There has never been a time when French authors have been so widely studied, so freely translated as at the present. Not an editor of a serious magazine but feels that an article on the newest French poet or novelist forms an essential feature of his monthly equipment. It is as indispensable as soup at a dinner-party. Unfortunately for our powers of discernment, not for long years has France been so poor in great men as at the present moment. She is passing through one of those periods of decadence and disease which have recurred more than once in her history. In politics, as well as in art and in literature, the need of a master hand is making itself felt. The great names which, in the middle of the century, made of Paris the Mecca of the artistic world, have passed away, and they have left no successors. Of this the British public remains all unconscious, and the study and admiration which thirty years ago we might have bestowed with advantage on Balzac and Flaubert, on Théophile Gautier and the de Goncourts, we bestow to-day in foolish abundance on Marcel Prévost and Anatole France, on Bourget and "Gyp."

The glamour with which, unconsciously, we are wont to invest all that is French in art and in literature makes it difficult to realise the extent to which France is shorn of her former glory. With the death last year of Puvis de Chavannes the generation of her great painters came to an end. When Daudet died a few months previously, his death seemed to mark the final disappearance of the past generation of her great writers. Daudet himself—as I have tried to show in this volume—was not a great writer. At his best he was not more than a charming *raconteur*, but he belonged to the period of greatness, a period that began with the romantics and died out in naturalism; he had imbibed something at least of its spirit; his house had been the daily *rendez-vous* of men of genius; he himself had been the intimate friend of Turgenev and Zola and the de Goncourts and many more. So it was perhaps excusable that his death should have called forth an outburst of laudatory lamentation, for which his personal gifts gave no warrant. He was a last link with a literary generation whom all France had reason to mourn. Of his intimates Zola alone remains, and Zola is no longer a living force in literature. To-day we may seek in vain for transcendent merit. Putting aside the young Franco-Belgian school, whose inspiration is in no way due to French sources, even though its members have elected to express themselves in the French language, and putting aside J. K. Huysmans, who, if he can be considered a Frenchman, is certainly a Frenchman of Dutch parentage, and who looms, a solitary mystical figure, above all his contemporaries, what is there in French literature of the present day beyond a flippant cleverness, and a desperate straining after effect? In a period of decadence man's artistic sense becomes as unbalanced as his moral sense. He loses his appreciation of what is sane and pure and true, and he craves for what is novel and sensational and meretricious. In France to-day, whether in art and in literature or in the drama, loud and garish effects are sought after; the desire is to startle rather than to please; and the most improbable and *outré* situations call forth the loudest applause. Readers of Maeterlinck will remember how, in one of the most illuminative of his essays, he observes that a great artist will refrain from painting scenes such as Marius destroying the Cimbri or the assassination of the Duke of Guise because he has realised that the psychology of murder and of victory is elementary and exceptional, and throws no light on the eternal mystery of life. It is of this fundamental truth that artists and novelists seem to be unconscious to-day. They 'place all the interest of their works in the violence of the anecdote which they reproduce.' And so we have the sanguinary horrors that hang year after year on the walls of the Salon; we have plays like *Cyrano de Bergerac* enjoying a phenomenal popularity; and we have a succession of novels depicting all that is most false and temporary and sensational in the society life of Paris eagerly devoured by readers on either side of the Channel. A sublime artist such as Turgenev is left unread and unhonoured, while critics enter into heated controversy over the rival merits of men whose very names will scarcely survive into the coming century.

We are all of us apt to be infected, in a measure, with the tastes and enthusiasms of our generation. It is only by comparing the objects of our immediate admiration with works of proved artistic merit that we can hope to arrive at a true estimate of their value. I confess that it was re-reading Turgenev's *On the Eve* in the very perfect translation that Mrs. Garnett has achieved for us, that forced upon me a fresh conviction of the artistic worthlessness of much that is accepted as admirable in the French fiction of to-day. And nothing seems to me to prove more conclusively the decadence of French taste than that in Paris, for so many years the adopted home of the Russian novelist, his fame should so quickly have fallen into abeyance, and that his work should be quite unfamiliar to the rising literary generation. That he should be equally unknown to the great mass of the British reading public is but one more proof that on questions of foreign literature we are content to follow the taste of the boulevards. And yet there has seldom been a story-teller so perfect in all respects as Turgenev. There is an entire unity of interest in his novels; they progress on simple, flowing lines; and on every page we discover fresh beauties of thought and diction. I know of no writer at once so profound and so slight, so full of deep feeling for those capable of discerning it, so pellucidly clear for those who merely ask to be amused. *On the Eve* is a story of daily life in a Russian family, but not for an instant does it sink into a mere record of domesticity. Straightway, in the opening chapter, in the talk of the two men, Turgenev plunges into the whole mystery of life, into its essential principles. It gives the note to the whole book, and it is done with an inimitable lightness of touch. Even where he is apparently dealing with the trivial and the commonplace, he brings all into harmony with his essential purpose. He is able, in a few half-enigmatical phrases, to confer on Uvar Ivanovitch, the fat, somnolent cousin of the Stahov family, a strange spiritual significance. Think what such a portrait would have been traced by the pen of a Zola! But in Turgenev's picture of the fat man there is nothing repulsive—rather an impressive sense of latent power, a vision of the great Russian people, which is still sleeping, and whose nature we in the West have never fathomed.

And Elena! Where else have we so delightful a heroine? She is a wonderful study of pure passionate girl nature, of one whose eyes are opened through love to the full comprehension of life. Turgenev has chosen to delineate the most difficult moment of all—the dawning of womanhood in a virgin soul under the stress of a great emotion—and his psychology is so sure, so unerring, that we gaze into the depths of Elena's soul as into a clear pool. The little retrospect of her girlhood—and, as a rule, there is nothing more tedious in novels—is unrivalled in its delicate unfolding of character. Elena is drawn on human, not on heroic lines; Turgenev had no need to paint her as a type of perfect womanhood. She captivates us by her transparent honesty, her noble aspirations; and the very faults of her youth, her pride, her intolerance of pettiness, her utter disregard of conventional prudence, only endear her to us the more. Her love for Insarov is the one real and true thing in her home circle, and so it sweeps all before it. No carefully concerted complications are allowed to intervene between her desire and its realisation. Turgenev was too great an artist to stoop to trivial contrivances for heightening the interest of his story. There are other suitors for Elena's hand—

Shubin, Bersenyev, and the practical Kurnatovsky—but they do not fight duels or hatch vengeful plots in the approved style of melodrama. They submit to fate, as the vast majority of mankind submits under similar circumstances. The volatile Shubin turns off his disappointment with a jest, and Bersenyev toils for the success of his friend and rival, realising that, in his own words, 'to put oneself in the second place is the whole significance of our life.' Of Insarov himself it has been customary to speak as one of Turgenev's few artistic failures. None of Turgenev's male characters, with the exception perhaps of Basarov, can compare in creative force with his women. He was essentially a delineator of feminine nature. But as far as Insarov is concerned, I think he is precisely what the Russian novelist intended him to be. Insarov is no hero—save in Elena's imagination—and Turgenev is fully aware of it. He has put into Shubin's mouth an accurate estimate of his character. It is far more true to feminine nature that Elena should have flung away her life and her home for one who, in all the qualities of the soul, was vastly her inferior. But in the white heat of her love she was able to kindle a corresponding glow in his heart; and it is on the lover of Elena, and not on the rigid narrow-souled patriot, that we finally bestow our sympathy. The tragedy of the closing scene is lessened by the tender beauty of the Venetian setting. It is not the intention of the novelist to harrow our feelings, but rather to show us the fundamental tragedy of life with all the compensations that love and youth and beauty bestow upon it.

Every one can see at a glance how simple and how sane the story is. It captivates by its transparent truth; it has no violent effects to offer to jaded literary appetites. *Une Nichée de Gentilshommes* even more than *On the Eve* is a tragedy of daily life. It is pervaded by a sense of Lisa's passion for Lavretski, but there is no adventure, no crisis, no result. For a brief moment the souls of Lavretski and of Lisa are brought face to face—then they drift apart, severed by their consciences, Lisa to a convent, Lavretski to a solitary old age. The conclusion would be almost banal were it not so convincingly true. Every character in the book, even to the least important, is portrayed with a rare delicacy of perception. Lisa herself is a more ethereal creation than Elena—we realise her less, but to many she will appeal almost more. Where Elena boldly seizes life with both hands, and accepts at once its joys and its sorrows, Lisa shrinks back and turns aside and guards her virginal purity to the end. They stand as types of two opposing ideals of womanhood—the active and the passive. They are true for all time, more true even than Shakespeare's women, and to have created them is the test of the pre-eminent artist.

Re-reading Turgenev after a lapse of many years, nothing has impressed me so much as the unique distinction he acquired through that very simplicity of style, which in earlier years one regarded almost as a defect. In truth, it is his simplicity which stands in the way of his popularity. To the average reader, his style is bare and chill. He never condescends to be gracefully ornate; above all, he is never grandiloquent. It requires a certain measure of literary appreciation to discover that his simplicity is not the result of poverty of imagination, but that it is the outcome of the very highest art. Take the chapter in *On the Eve*, which is devoted to the apparently trivial episode of the expedition to Tsaritsino, one of those troublesome *parties de plaisir* on which Anna Vassilyevna set her heart at stated intervals. The picnic passes off in a perfectly prosaic manner, and related by the ordinary novelist, it would have absolutely no significance. But Turgenev, while confining himself within the limits of an almost bald recital, describes the scene with such delicate irony, with such illuminating conviction, that the discerning reader would not sacrifice a page of it. Only a great artist can dare to be so natural, so unadorned, so neglectful of all the little resources of his profession. It is undeniable that Turgenev arrives at more vivid effects, at a more convincing presentation by his reticence of speech than novelists who exhaust all the technical possibilities of their craft. Gabriele D'Annunzio, for example, will surround his central love-motive with a wealth of sensual detail intended to enhance the effect of the passion. But is there anything in the *Trionfo della Morte* more convincing than Lisa's love for Lavretski, or Elena's passionate self-surrender to Insarov? And yet in each case the climax is described in but a few lines, with an absolute chastity of expression. Unhappily, the novel-reading public does not see this, and longs for literary frills and furbelows, just as the average Englishwoman does not see that the simplest frock confectioned by a great Paris modiste is of higher value than the most sumptuous satin gown from Regent Street.

There are critics who treat Turgenev as a political pamphleteer, and extract his views on Nihilism and on the future of his country from the characters in his novels. So, too, there are distinguished critics of Dante who seem to overlook the fact that the Florentine was perhaps the greatest poet of all time, in their anxiety to establish his precise opinion concerning some unimportant political event of his day. In either case, the attempt is exceedingly futile. I venture to think Turgenev's political views are a matter of small import, and so I prefer *On the Eve* and *A House of Gentlefolk* to *Virgin Soil* or *Fathers and Sons*. What is essential is that he was an admirable artist and a most perfect tale-teller, with a facility derived perhaps from the East, that East which still exercises so potent an influence over the Slav race. Would that French tale-tellers of to-day would take the great Scythian as their model! But he is too sane, too simple for public taste in a period of decadence. Nor, indeed, even if they would, is there any one in France to-day who could write as Turgenev wrote. Artists reproduce what is highest and noblest and most ideal in the aspirations of their time and nation. Great literatures belong to periods of ardent faith, of a passionate love of liberty, of national growth and expansion. If a people's aspirations are centred even for a time on base and unworthy objects, great artists will be sought for in vain. And so, in the place of the giants of a previous generation, we find installed to-day as popular favourites the authors of *Aphrodite* and *Demi-Vierges*, and *L'Année de Clarisse*.

Paul Adam, perhaps better than any one else, may stand as a type of the second-rate French novelist of the moment. He produces a novel with great regularity every three months. He made his *début* some years ago as a writer in the de Goncourt style, in language so bizarre and involved as to be almost incomprehensible. To-day he has somewhat modified his linguistic methods, and not long ago he achieved a considerable success with *L'Année de Clarisse.* It is, I frankly admit, the only volume of Paul Adam that has come into my hands. It is sufficient for my purpose. From a cursory perusal, I confess to have retained no impressions save those of bewilderment and disgust. The book professes to describe a year in the life of a little third-rate actress engaged at some French watering-place. It is a history of her amours, her toilettes, and the doings of her *petite chienne* Love. Into the story, *pêle-mêle*, without any sort of order or sequence, the author has flung the most *outré* and sensational episodes in his repertory; duels, bull-fights, scenes in a mad-house, mingled with all the cabals, jealousies, and sordid intrigues of stage-life. There are a bewildering number of characters, but there is no attempt at characterisation. For all practical purposes, the book has no beginning and no end, and no conceivable reason for having been written save that of piling one horror on another, of unmasking vice in all its repulsive details, of surpassing its predecessors in vulgarity. It is for these very reasons that *L'Année de Clarisse* has been welcomed in Paris as M. Paul Adam's most noteworthy production.

One looks round almost in vain for symptoms of a coming revival. Huysmans alone stands aloft, a strange prophetic figure; but it is barely half a decade since Huysmans himself trod the road to Damascus, and it is yet too early to sum up his ultimate influence on his nation's literature. Hitherto, so far as I know, he has called up no imitators. Maeterlinck, who has been, after Huysmans, the greatest exponent of the Symbolist movement, seemed at one time likely to herald a new dramatic era in Paris. But Maeterlinck is in no sense a Frenchman, and already his influence in the French capital is on the wane.

The sudden enthusiasm he called forth was but the caprice of a moment among a people who, even more than the Athenians of old, are ever clamouring for some new thing. A study of the pages of the *Mercure de France*, that happy hunting-ground of *les jeunes*, hardly convinces one of the creative genius of the rising literary generation. They have more audacity than talent, and their imaginative gifts lead them at times into very questionable fields. For the rest, the accepted representatives of French fiction pursue their accustomed course with no prospect of any change. Zola, having brought to a close his wearisome Trilogy, which emphasised all the artistic faults of his earlier work, has plunged into a new and lengthy novel of serious purpose, with the unpromising title of *Fécondité*. M. Bourget still adheres to his elaborate studies of conjugal infidelity in aristocratic circles, widely read by the society of which he writes. M. Pierre Loti has published some charming and vivid impressions of the Holy Land; but even amid the stirring thoughts that a visit to Jerusalem must call up in the minds of the least impressionable among us, he has not been able to escape from the obsession of his own *blasé* personality, which in so many disguises has been the centre of all his books. Yet in *Ramuntcho*, his recent idyl of the Basque country, it is but fair to say that he has struck once again a deeper human note, the note which will make *Pêcheurs d'Islande* live when all the Aziyadés, and Fatougayes, and Madame Chrysanthèmes of his volumes of travel are long since forgotten. Loti, more than almost any one, has all his life been a seeker after what is novel and bizarre; and his art has consisted mainly in drawing a piquant contrast between the ennui bred of his own hyper-civilisation, and the primitive emotions of the women of strange races with whom he has entered into ephemeral relations. Yet, there are pages which show beyond a doubt that in Loti there is something deeper than a mere facile gift for description; and that, had he passed his literary apprenticeship in a more robust school than is to be found in France at present, he might have turned his talents to higher purpose.

Here and there, it is true, attempts are being made—doubtless in good faith—to cast out the extravagant and the unreal, and to paint once again the simple scenes of man's daily existence. The attempt has been made, among others, by M. Anatole France, that prince of dilettantism, whose habitual assumption of a refined scepticism has unhappily given the tone to young writers of far slenderer gifts than his own. In *L'Orme du Mail,* vaunted to the skies by his friends, M. France has essayed to reproduce the atmosphere, the sentiment, the poetry of a narrow provincial and cathedral city. But how thin and trivial and inconclusive is the result! Not for one moment does he penetrate beneath the outer crust of petty interests—the jealousies between the Bishop and the Préfet, between clerical and anti-clerical. It is the work of a man uninspired by any noble ideal, bereft of all large humanity. Flaubert would have made of the subject a study of convincing veracity. Turgenev would have transformed it into an exquisite idyl. As it is, *L'Orme du Mail* seems to me almost unreadably dull.

I have sometimes thought that women are largely to blame for the present decadence in literary taste, which in France has followed closely upon the general inclusion of women into the ranks of the reading public. The taste of the idle woman of the upper and middle classes cannot fail to exercise a determining influence in the book market. She is the prop of the circulating library, that approved method for the rapid dissemination of inferior literature. Women have never been great readers of Balzac or of Flaubert; very few could pass an examination in the characters of the *Comédie Humaine*; but they are insatiable readers of Bourget and Marcel Prévost. And in this respect, Englishwomen are no whit superior to their French sisters. A book has only to be in French, and to be what is usually spoken of as 'improper,' in order to be read with an avidity which its merits do not in the least warrant, and which would probably not be aroused by English novels of an equally low literary level. It requires no courage to be audacious when so-called 'audacity' is the one thing needful to ensure the success of an otherwise worthless book. The market for foreign books in England is exceedingly large, and French writers are, more and more, addressing themselves to a cosmopolitan audience. Thus, blame from beyond the sea would prove as potent a deterrent as blame from home. Hitherto, we in England have given direct encouragement to the most decadent of recent tendencies in French literature, and we have been curiously unappreciative of those great qualities which placed her earlier novelists far above our own. With a Pharisaism not altogether strange to us, we have prided ourselves in public on the purity of our own literature, whilst feasting in private on the pruriency of our neighbour's.

It is pleasant to remember that France, more than any other nation, is endowed with an inexhaustible recuperative power. Over and over again she has emerged triumphant from disasters that might well have overwhelmed a people of less buoyant temperament. It is as true of her in an artistic as in a political sense. To-day, she may possess no men of transcendent merit; but for aught we know, she may already be on the eve of a new Renaissance, which in the early years of the coming century may restore to her her pre-eminence in art and in letters. The reasonable and logical explanations which are forthcoming to account for recognised social phenomena only cover a very small part of the ground when the question at issue is the existence or absence of great men. In the birth of genius there enters an element far beyond human understanding. Who can explain the sudden appearance of a Dante or a Shakespeare? Even at the present day French critics uphold, not unworthily, her saner traditions; and with M. Brunetière and M. de Vogüé on the one hand, and M. Jules Lemaître on the other, we have the assurance of sound and serious literary criticism which cannot fail to bear fruit. And so I refrain from gloomy predictions; and while chronicling with regret that for the moment her craftsmen show themselves so destitute of talent, I continue to cherish an indulgent affection for all that comes to us from the French nation.

CYRANO DE BERGERAC

IT is a suggestive fact for all who make a study of French literature that the year in which the long Dreyfus agitation reached its climax is also that in which Edmond Rostand attained to an unprecedented success with his play *Cyrano de Bergerac*. Dreyfus and *Cyrano* give the note of the past year in France; nothing else will survive. The same public that hissed Zola and cheered Esterhazy outside the *Palais de Justice* has applauded *Cyrano* night after night all through the year at the Porte St. Martin theatre. The two manifestations are but different aspects of one and the same popular conviction. The sentiment which permeates M. Rostand's drama, and which Cyrano sums up with his dying breath in the exclamation 'Mon panache!' is identical with that which has driven the French General Staff to shield, at all costs, the so-called 'honour of the army.' In either case we are dealing with the expression of one of the fundamental characteristics of the French nation, with the outcome of the triumph of militarism. On the stage we see it in its romantic, chivalrous setting; in the Court of Law in its modern materialistic results.

This—and not, as people have assumed, its transcendent literary merit—is the true explanation of the popularity enjoyed by M. Rostand's play. Its chief claim on our attention lies in the fact that it appeared at so à propos a moment. Our literature, of necessity, is the expression of our national ideals and aspirations; and in painting the supremacy of a fantastic militarism, tinged with 'romantic' idealism, M. Rostand has been the mouthpiece of all the frustrated desire after military ascendency which has fretted the Third Republic throughout its existence. On his patriotic side every Frenchman nurses something of the *Cyrano* spirit. The love of military glory lies at the very root of his character. Henri IV. and Napoleon are the true heroes of his choice. The triumph of the *panache*, the flaunting of the white plume unsullied in the face of a discomfited foe, for this the French people has sighed in vain during thirty years on the field of international politics, and this it has acclaimed with frenzy when glorified on the dramatic stage. *Cyrano de Bergerac* has appealed to the whole nation, and it has found an echo in every French heart. Even austere critics like M. E. Faguet have so far lost their sense of proportion as to pronounce it the finest dramatic poem of the last half-century, and it has been hailed on every side as the herald of a new dramatic dawn.

But all this does not necessarily make *Cyrano* a masterpiece, any more than the most successful music-hall ditty ever sung is necessarily good music. Indeed, had it been in truth a great play, its success would have been far less rapid than has been the case. For a great play means surely one that appeals to our highest intelligence, to our deepest moral conscience. It is a play whose whole significance could not possibly be grasped at first sight by the ordinary theatre-going public —else were the intelligence of the ordinary public on a par with that of the author—and which would certainly give rise to much searching controversy concerning its intention and execution. If *Hamlet* could be thrust suddenly, without the magic of Shakespeare's name, on the British public, does any one believe for a moment that it would enjoy instantaneous and universal recognition as a work of supreme genius? Ibsen is the nearest approach to Shakespeare that the contemporary world can show, and we all know how Ibsen has been derided and misinterpreted, and what a limited measure of popular recognition has been accorded to his plays when they have been placed upon the stage. Maeterlinck has fared even worse; and when from time to time some discerning manager has given material form to his delicate spiritual evocations, the attempt has earned little more from the general public than an amiable toleration. In many quarters his mystical dramas have merely excited derision as grotesque and meaningless pantomime. Henrik Ibsen and Maurice Maeterlinck, alone of modern dramatists, and on lines far removed from one another, have attempted to widen the narrow sphere of dramatic action, to abandon the external and the circumstantial, and to bring upon the stage the eternal mystery of life. They have probed, each in his own way, far deeper than any of their contemporaries, into the secrets of the human soul, into that spiritual region which lies so close behind the visible surface of life, but of whose very existence so few of us seem conscious. They alone can claim to have pointed the way towards a new period of dramatic efflorescence; and if, indeed, the coming century were destined to usher in a great dramatic revival, I do not see how its exponents could fail to owe much to the genius of the Fleming and the Norseman. I honestly believe that a time will come when *Ghosts* and *The Wild Duck* on the one hand, and *La Princesse Maleine* on the other, will enjoy as full a measure of popular appreciation as has been bestowed in our own day on the plays of Robertson or Pinero. It is impossible not to believe that the world will some day awake to the beauty of writing so truthful and so convincing. But our public taste must first undergo a long period of educational enlightenment. Meanwhile, it is perhaps inevitable that we should attempt to discern the germs of that dramatic renaissance which, in a dim way, we all feel to be needful, in works like *The Second Mrs. Tanqueray* and *Cyrano de Bergerac*.

It may then be taken for granted that M. Rostand has not produced a work of any revolutionary tendency. *Cyrano* marks no turning-point in the history of dramatic literature. What M. Rostand has accomplished has been pointed out by M. Jules Lemaître in an article which is the one piece of sane and sober criticism that has appeared on the subject during the past year. '*Cyrano*,' writes the most accomplished of contemporary French critics, ' prolongs and combines with originality and brilliancy three centuries of fantastic comedy and moral grace of a very French order.' The play is, in a sense, a recapitulation of everything that has inspired the French stage from its first inception ; it has affinities with the work of every playwright from Corneille to the elder Dumas. It is not a psychological play ; it does not profess to touch on any of the deeper tragedies of human existence, and so it cannot be classed, for good or evil, among the characteristic products of our later nineteenth century. Its interest is entirely retrospective; it carries us back to a time beloved of novelists and dramatists—the time of Richelieu and Louis xiii. With the plot every one is familiar. It rests on an antithesis—on the nobility of Cyrano's soul contrasted with the plainness of his person, on the delicacy of his passion counterbalanced by the abnormal length of his nose. Even here M. Rostand cannot claim to originality of conception, for in making use of startling contradictions in the character of his hero as the pivot of his drama he is merely following in the footsteps of Victor Hugo.

From the very outset of the play it becomes clear that the spectator has been borne aloft into the realms of etherealised romance. The piece is rightly described as a heroic comedy, for it marks the very acme of the sentimental heroism of the early years of the seventeenth century—the sentiment which inspired Mlle. de Scudéri's *Pays du Tendre*, and which had its most graceful and emotional advocates among the *habitués* of the Hotel de Rambouillet. From that standpoint—and M. Rostand's greatest merit is that he adopts the standpoint with an unerring effect—nothing could be more noble and beautiful, nothing more *attendrissant* than Cyrano's love for his cousin Roxane. It seems brutal to suggest that a little honest commonsense could have put an end, at a stroke, to the heartrending situation, and that Cyrano and his cousin might have enjoyed fourteen years of conjugal happiness with a perfectly clear conscience. For then we should have lost the dying Alexandrines, and the final wave of *mon panache*, in which the artificial *motif* of the drama finds its supreme expression.

For my part, the worship of the *panache* presents few attractions, and so I have not been able to feel that admiration for the character of Cyrano which has been so freely bestowed by the French nation. The whole *motif* of the play is to me radically false, and consequently lacking in any permanent interest. Yet it were unfair to deny that Rostand himself has realised the complex character of his hero thoroughly, and has drawn him in vigorous and unmistakable lines. His heroism may frequently verge on the ridiculous; but, at least, he is a personage of flesh and blood, and he represents an ideal which, in a society imbued with militarism, exercises an unfailing fascination. He is a first cousin to d'Artagnan, pre-eminent among all 'bretteurs et menteurs sans vergogne,' with a voluptuous melancholy superimposed, which adds incalculably to his popularity. And for d'Artagnan, most readers of Dumas have a warm corner in their hearts. So I can conceive that Cyrano, boaster and brawler though he be, will be treasured up by many as an attractive type of human sinner. He will live, as most of Dickens' characters live, thanks to the fact that he is a caricature rather than a portrait; that he is all on the surface, without atmosphere and without mystery, and is therefore perfectly comprehensible to the average intelligence. To conclude, however, from the definiteness with which Cyrano stands before us, that the author can lay claim to skill as a delineator of character, would be a very grave mistake. There is no characterisation in any of M. Rostand's earlier work; and putting aside Cyrano, there is none in the play by which he has made his reputation. Ragueneau merely supplies the comic element which, in one form or another, is considered an indispensable adjunct of every play. And his confectioner's shop serves as an effective variety in the scenes. De Bret, de Guiche, the duenna, the friar, are all conceived on conventional stage lines; they are mechanical puppets, with no personality of their own, contrived in order to help forward the action of the play. Roxane is a nonentity, a *précieuse* who is captivated first by the *beaux yeux* of Christian, and then by the high-flown sentiments of Cyrano. That she should have remained a widow for fourteen years out of devotion to the dead Christian, strikes one rather as an inexplicable caprice than an act of heroic devotion, so little does she convey any sense of passion in the fourth Act. Of de Neuvillette there is nothing to say; he is without life or soul; and yet for any one who is alive to the hidden workings of the human character there should have been much to attract and inspire in a study of a silent, sensitive youth realising that the love of his life is being dragged from him by some magnetic influence, of whose nature he is ignorant. But amid the din and the bustle and the fighting which make up the first four acts of the comedy, there is neither time nor space for gazing into the human soul, for penetrating the mysteries of the human heart. M. Rostand has not attempted the task; all his energies have been concentrated on the outward adornment of his central figure.

Yet in spite of this very serious lack, M. Rostand possesses many qualifications for writing a play of the type of *Cyrano de Bergerac*, steeped as it is in seventeenth century romanticism. For the first time his talents have full scope, and his very defects are not without their value. M. Rostand is not a great poet; there is not a line that will live either in *La Princesse Lointaine* or in *La Samaritaine*. But he possesses in a high degree a capacity for facile versification, the talent for expressing anything and everything in rhyme. He is full of buoyant spirits; he has the southern gift for florid expansiveness of expression. There are affinities between his nature and Daudet's, a touch of gay insouciance and irrepressible verve which recalls the early work of the author of *Tartarin*. The inherent dignity of the Alexandrine is smoothed down by the dramatist into something almost frivolous in its easy flow. The characters positively chatter in twelve-syllable verse. As a poet he has always been tinged with 'preciosity'—in *La Samaritaine* it jars upon the reader almost in every line—but in the present instance to be 'precious' in his choice of language is to be in harmony with his subject. His ingenious conceits and exaggerated metaphors — so happily described by Lemaître as 'd'un mauvais goût délectable,' run riot on every page. Cyrano's famous tirade to de Guiche on his own nose is a *tour de force* in audacious repartee and long-drawn-out humour, which entitles the author to a foremost place as a writer—not of poetry —but of mock heroics. And no one will deny to the ballad of the *Cadets de Gascogne* a great measure of that swing and rhythm and jovial characteristic sentiment of which French poetry has perhaps fewer examples than English, and which we ourselves value at so exorbitant a rate in the poems of Mr. Rudyard Kipling. So, too, his admirers would certainly be able to pick out a score and more of passages written with a jingling dexterity and ready Gallic wit which are not without their charm. He is an adept at quick retort, flinging the ball of repartee backwards and forwards with an enviable promptitude. But when we come to the passages in the play on which M. Rostand's claims as a serious poet would naturally rest — the dying lines spoken by Cyrano, the long-drawn-out balcony episode, the last scene between Roxane and de Neuvillette on the battle-field—the artificiality both of sentiment and language excludes the author from any right to a place in the front rank. I fail to discern either depth, or grandeur, or passion in his verse. I know all that has been written in France by distinguished critics of the grace and beauty of Cyrano's appeal to Roxane from beneath the balcony. The scene when read leaves me absolutely unmoved, and on the stage it is intolerably lengthy. Compare it for an instant —as every English reader instinctively does compare it—to the balcony scene in *Romeo and Juliet*, and the superficial sentimentality of the one stands convicted by the passion of the other. Even when the long preliminary interchange of elegant futilities is over, and Cyrano is supposed to be pouring out his heart for the first and only time to the love of his life, the author cannot rise above the language of a *petit-maître*. His conventional mannerisms still cling around him, stifling the ring of true passion. There is nothing in the whole passage more convincing than the rather graceful fancy about the jessamine spray—

> 'Car tu trembles! car j'ai senti, que tu le veuilles
> Ou non, le tremblement adoré de ta main
> Descendre tout le long des branches du jasmin!'

Nothing more soul-stirring than the string of ingenious conceits on the significance of a kiss, culminating in the much quoted line—

> 'Un point rose qu'on met sur l'i du verbe aimer.'

Compare it, in its elaborate preciosity, with Romeo's parting word to Juliet—

> 'I would I were thy bird.'

And Juliet's reply—

> 'Sweet, so would I.
> Yet I should kill thee with much cherishing.'

And we are saved from any further danger of mistaking the tinsel for pure gold.

After the fourth Act, which slips at its close into something perilously resembling melodrama, we find ourselves back in the fifth Act in the rarefied atmosphere of an exalted romanticism. The worldly Roxane has mourned her lover for fourteen years in a Paris convent —a few conventional stage nuns compounded of primness and simplicity are introduced to lend an air of reality to the scene—and the faithful Cyrano comes every Saturday to give her the gossip of the week. On this occasion, in an unnaturally deliberate manner, Roxane never looks at her old friend in order that she may not discover till the crucial moment that he has had his head cut open by a log of wood dropped on it by an enemy. Roxane gives him to read the last letter written to her by Christian, which for fourteen years she has carried daily next her heart; and Cyrano, not to be outdone in fidelity, remembers every word of it—after fourteen years!—and recites it aloud in the dusk. And Roxane, penetrated by his voice, discovers the truth, discovers that it is he, and not Christian, who wrote the letter, and that by loving the writer she has unconsciously been loving him. Then it is time for Cyrano to die. His friends hurry in; he says everything that there is to say when you wish to die in as impressive a manner as possible; he stands with his back to a tree making wild passes at imaginary foes, 'les Compromis, les Préjugés, les Lâchetés,' and draws his last breath after assuring his audience that he will appear at the gates of heaven without a stain on 'mon panache'! It is, more than anything else, this final tableau that has evoked the delirious enthusiasm of the French nation. Cyrano, in his death, is symbolical of all that France aspires after, all to which she is conscious that she has not attained. The unreality, the grotesqueness of the scene pass unheeded, and in a period of *déchéance*, and disappointment, and wounded vanity the French people derive consolation from the dramatic representation of their national ideals. To them, *Cyrano* will remain a great play, because through *Cyrano* they have spoken to the world.

La Princesse Lointaine, produced some four years ago by Sarah Bernhardt at the Renaissance Theatre, is written in a not less romantic vein, but with the military *motif* entirely excluded. It is an attempt to resuscitate the spirit that produced the Crusades and the Courts of Love and all the tender emotional ideals of mediæval chivalry. The troubadour, Joffroy Rudel, is sick of love for the Princess Melissinde of Tripoli, of whose wondrous beauty pilgrims have brought word to France. He starts on the long journey in search of her, and arrives in a dying condition before Tripoli. His friend Bertrand undertakes to plead his cause with the Princess, and she mistakes Bertrand for the troubadour himself, whose songs in her honour have touched her heart. For a brief moment they resolve to live for each other and to forget Rudel; then nobler instincts prevail, and they hurry to the ship, and the poet dies happy in his lady's arms. Bertrand joins the Crusade, and Melissinde retires to Mount Carmel. The little play is not without charm and grace, but it represents a state of feeling too remote from actual conditions for it to appeal to a French public, and, unlike *Cyrano*, it has no connecting link with modern idols. In manner it is too purely imitative, and the artificiality of the inspiration is everywhere apparent, while the author had not acquired that mastery of the technique of his craft to which a certain share in the success of the later play must be attributed. Whatever the cause, *La Princesse Lointaine* excited but little interest, and it was reserved to *Cyrano* to lift the young poet of a sudden to the very pinnacle of social success.

It follows from all I have said that M. Rostand's play will never be greatly appreciated by foreign readers. In Italy, where the artistic instincts of the public are far more trustworthy than with us, it has been received with coldness and indifference. In England, as we habitually take our drama, our art and our fiction from Paris, so we were prepared also to take *Cyrano*, and many of us hastened to acclaim it as a great and noble work of art. As the French have not discovered for themselves that *Cyrano* is not a great play, it was hardly to be expected that our English critics should discover it for them. Mr. Gosse bestowed upon it the sanction of his deliberate approval; and a critic in the *Nineteenth Century*, with a rashness of which I think he must already repent, declared it to be one of the most remarkable plays ever seen on any stage in any age, and that nothing in Corneille, Racine, Molière, or Victor Hugo deserved to be placed on the same level. We still assume in public that M. Rostand's play is a masterpiece, but in reality its actual success on this side of the channel was of short duration. Honest people admitted that they found it tedious on the stage, and I do not imagine that its readers have been numerous outside a small literary coterie.

But there is an aspect of what may be termed the *Cyrano* craze, not without interest for ourselves. In France the military chauvinism of the moment declares itself in heroic comedy; in England a corresponding sentiment finds expression in military ballads. If France has her Rostand craze, we have our Kipling craze. Neither has its origin in a love of art or of literature. Within the last few years a great wave of Imperialism, gathering force as it advanced, has passed over the country. And with this spread of Imperialist ideas there has synchronised among us an outburst of patriotic and political and military song in which the aspirations of the nation find an outlet. Mr. Newbolt has sung our fleet in *Admirals All*; books of the nature of Fitchett's *Fights for the Flag*, which appeal frankly to the fighting instincts of the people, have sold literally by the tens of thousands; and, above all, Tommy Atkins has found a poetic champion in the person of Mr. Rudyard Kipling. I am not myself quite sure whether Mr. Kipling is cause or effect—whether we are Imperialist because we are nourished on *Barrack-room Ballads*; or whether, being Imperialist, the ballads appeal to us with such soul-stirring effect. But it is indisputable that one of the notes of the lighter literature of our day is a militant patriotism which cannot fail to exercise an influence on the public mind. We have been told with so much emphasis, and on so many occasions, that Mr. Kipling's poems are literature, that it is clear there must still be a lingering doubt in many minds as to whether, after all, they are not merely music-hall ditties. But granting they are literature, granting *Cyrano de*

Bergerac is literature, are they of the literature that will live permanently in the history of a nation? Here, I think, the answer is in the negative. It is always difficult to appraise works of the moment at their true value, but it may almost be taken as a guiding rule that posterity will never endorse the enthusiastic verdicts of contemporaries. People will admire a patriotic song for reasons similar to those which prompt them to admire a hymn, reasons which have no relation whatever to the artistic value of the verse. And it is where matters entirely extraneous to art are allowed to modify our artistic opinions, that the latter are most certain to stand in need of subsequent revision. It is quite conceivable that earlier in the century 'Ye Mariners of England' and 'The Burial of Sir John Moore' excited as much lavish commendation as the 'Recessional' or the lines on 'Bobs' excite to-day. It may even be that Dibdin and Wolfe were held in many circles in greater esteem than Shelley or Keats. Have we confirmed the judgments of our ancestors? And will our grandchildren confirm our own when they realise that towards the close of the nineteenth century Mr. Rudyard Kipling was held in higher honour by the great British public than Algernon Swinburne? I take it that patriotic poetry, like historical painting, must usually occupy a rather humble place in the artistic scale. I distinguish here between patriotism and love of liberty, between the glorification of your own country at the expense of another, and the aspiration on behalf of your country of a measure of freedom without which there can be no national growth. The one is merely an extended egotism; the other is one of the most powerful instincts that rule humanity. Unfortunately, it is a chauvinistic patriotism which prevails in England and France to-day, and experience goes to prove that chauvinism is not productive of permanent works of art. And so I believe that to a future generation the poems of Mr. Kipling in England, and the plays of M. Rostand in France, will be interesting, not as illustrative of the Art of the century, but as exemplifying the fascination exercised over the public mind by those who have the good fortune to interpret the transitory emotions of their time and their country.

ALPHONSE DAUDET

THE friend of Flaubert and Turgenev, of the de Goncourts and de Maupassant, Alphonse Daudet survived all his contemporaries in literature save only Zola. He was but fifty-seven at his death, yet even in his lifetime he had come to be numbered with a past generation of writers. Literary ideals in Paris are swift in their growth, still swifter in their decay. Daudet knew nothing of symbolism or of mysticism; he never wrote a single psychological page. Thus he belongs unmistakably to the middle, and not to the close, of our century. By his natural gifts he might have identified himself either with realism or with romanticism, for he combined to an unusual extent a keen imaginative sense with a remarkable power of observation. And indeed he has frequently been claimed as an adherent by the exponents of both these rival schools of thought. In reality Daudet belonged to no definite school of fiction, nor has he left any disciples. He was a subtle blend of the Provençal and the Parisian, and the main characteristics of his writing could neither be taught nor acquired. Of himself Daudet used to speak as an improvisator, a troubadour. He was endowed as a birthright with the Provençal gift of song; and although the author of *Les Prunes* and *Les Amoureuses* wrote few verses after his twentieth year, it is his lyrical gift that permeates his prose with much of its undeniable grace. In his youth a dreamer and a poet, and a passionate lover of all that is beautiful in life, he became in later years more and more absorbed in the study of human existence amid the hideous accessories and the demoralising influences of a great city. The naturalist movement laid its spell upon him as upon most of his contemporaries, and for a time he deliberately drilled his vagrant fancies to the tedious reproduction of aspects of life with which his essential nature was entirely out of harmony. Yet in spite of this lamentable misconception of his art, he remained to the end of his life a true Meridional, with all the vivacity, the *bonhomie*, the irrepressible optimism of the sunny southern temperament.

In a nature so volatile as that of Daudet, it is not easy to analyse clearly the component parts, nor of writing so various as that of the *Lettres de mon Moulin* and—let us say—*Les Rois en Exil*, to indicate the permanent characteristics. Contrasts lie generally more on the surface than points of contact. But taking Daudet's work as a whole, I am inclined to say that his greatest gift was his gift of pleasing, of all literary qualities at once the most impalpable and the most real. At his best he was so charming a writer that he almost became a great one. The most sordid subjects are invested by him with a certain grace; the most unworthy character depicted by his pen retains an irresistible claim upon our affections. With the uncritical world Daudet enjoyed a popularity to which neither a Flaubert nor a Balzac has ever attained. His novels ran quickly through dozens of editions; wealth came as the final seal to his triumph. And yet it would not be fair to say that he did not wholly deserve the European success that he enjoyed. Although the result may have been unequal, Daudet was at all times a diligent and conscientious writer, giving of his best, and not —consciously at least—playing to the gallery. In his early garret days in Paris, with starvation held barely at arm's length, he persistently refused to earn an easy competence by prostituting his pen to boulevard journalism, nor would he ever risk deterioration in the literary form of the *Contes* that de Villemessant gladly accepted for the *Figaro* by recklessly multiplying their production. The charm reflected in his works lay in the man himself, and earned for him a host of friends and an unclouded domestic life—it lay in his open, sunny, inconsequent, southern nature, with his quick sympathies, his irony at once forcible and delicate, his ready tears. It lay in the spontaneousness of his talent, in his Provençal gift of improvisation. One seems to feel, at least in his earlier work, that he wrote from the very necessities of his nature, as the lark sings, unencumbered by theories concerning his art or by doctrinaire views on methods of composition. And it lay, too, in what was an essential characteristic of his nature, his rapid alternation of mood. Take even the slightest of his *Contes*, *La Chèvre de M. Seguin* or *Les Vieux* in the *Lettres de mon Moulin*, or any of his sketches of the Franco-Prussian War. Within a few pages he is in turn sad, gay, sentimental, ironical, pathetic, and one mood glides into the next without jar or friction. And so he seldom wearies his readers, their attention is always kept on the alert; one reads with a constant pleasing sense of the unexpected in thought or phrase. Daudet all through his life was an attractive personality, and the popularity of his books was inextricably bound up with himself. His very appearance accorded with the popular ideal of a bohemian genius. His well-cut features, his large liquid eyes, his black hair falling in loose locks over his forehead, locks which not even the official request of the Duc de Morny could induce him to cut, rendered him a conspicuously interesting figure. His life-size portrait by Carrière, the refined, melancholy face gazing out of a brown mist, was one of the sensations of the Champ de Mars Exhibition some half-dozen years ago. Daudet was always the spoilt child of fortune. The miseries of his childhood passed lightly over his genial nature, and his early struggles in Paris, if acute, were at least of short duration ; for the young poet was only in his twenty-first year when de Morny, acting at the request of the Empress, offered him a post in one of the Ministerial offices. From that time his livelihood was assured, and his verses, his good looks, and an Empress's patronage quickly laid the foundation of his thirty years' successful career as a novelist.

Judged simply as a charming and successful writer of *Contes*, Daudet deserves all the praise that has been bestowed upon him ; but if he is to be compared with the great creative novelists of the century—with Tolstoi, or with Turgenev, with Balzac, or with Flaubert—it becomes at once apparent that he stands on a lower plane. The mere suggestion of such comparison would be ludicrous were it not that the novelist himself in later life came to regard his vocation as a delineator of *mœurs Parisiennes* with so much solemnity, and that the outside world is apt to judge of a man's merit purely by the measure of his success. To many estimable persons the fact that *Tartarin de Tarascon* has sold by the hundred thousand, whereas the *Éducation Sentimentale* has never attained to popular recognition at all, appears as an irrefragable proof that the former is the greater book of the two. Daudet's limitations were the inevitable outcome of his qualities. All his work is on the surface. He sees all the colour, none of the mystery of life. He never once penetrates to its hidden meanings. Take his pathos, perhaps with the ordinary public the most popular of all his attributes. It is the pathos of a facile, emotional temperament quickly stirred to sorrow by those obvious calamities in life which appeal to even the least impressionable of onlookers. To Daudet his pathos was true and real, and it was invariably expressed with a charming ingenuousness; but it would be idle to pretend that he penetrated to—indeed, that he was ever conscious of— the intimate tragedy of life. A facile brilliancy of style is hardly compatible with a divining sense of *le dessous des choses.* If the eye is attracted and retained by external features, it stands to reason that it cannot also pierce beneath the surface. Daudet excelled in conveying impressions with extraordinary vividness. Nothing escaped his keen southern eye, his quick perceptions: the smallest detail was transferred with enthusiasm to his page. He belonged to the *plein air* school of impressionists. He loved garish colours and startling contrasts and hard sunshine. He was content to paint what he saw, without troubling himself as to its possible hidden significance. Readers of *Numa Roumestan* will remember the opening chapter describing the great public fête in the amphitheatre at Aps, Numa himself the central figure on the platform. Daudet gloried in such a scene. The dust, the glare, the crowd, the noisy applause of his beloved Provençaux are reproduced with an inimitable verve. He is carried away by what he himself termed *l'enflure méridionale,* of which he was not ashamed to own that he had his share.

Daudet lives entirely in the present. His

subjects are all chosen from contemporary French life. There is no trace in his writing of classic culture, or even of a general acquaintance with the literature of his own or of any other country. He relies for his material entirely upon his eyes. He notes what he sees, and he constructs his novels from the stores he has accumulated. The result is to give a curiously scattered, detached impression of life seen entirely from the outside. All his characters are constructed on the same principle. Their outer characteristics, their appearance, their attitudes, their gestures are painted with vivid realism ; every personage has his distinguishing trait ; we are shown their actions at certain moments in their lives ; we are familiar with their talk, their colloquialisms, their *patois*; but of their hidden life, of the motives which impel their conduct, of their spiritual consciousness we know literally nothing. The marvellous growth of the human soul swayed this way and that by intangible ever-contending influences is as a closed book to Daudet. Having conceived his characters under a certain aspect, he presents them under

the same aspect to the end of the chapter.
M. Jules Lemaître somewhere describes them
as 'de véridiques et vivantes marionnettes,' and
the phrase has always remained in my mind as
a peculiarly happy one. They are puppets of
which M. Daudet himself pulls the strings.
Yet, strange to say, it is by his characters that
he has become most famous. Bompard, Delobelle, Tartarin have been for years household
names in France, and form part of the literary
stock-in-trade of every journalist. The fact
is a testimony to Daudet's gift for seizing the
predominant external trait in a man's character,
and placing it in so vivid a light that the most
obtuse reader cannot fail to carry away the
desired impression. In other words, Daudet
was a caricaturist, not a character-painter ; and
Tartarin de Tarascon, the most notorious of his
creations, was the most obvious caricature of
them all. To have introduced the infinite
gradations of light and shade that go to make
up a real human portrait would, in his case,
have been merely to blur his outline, and
deprive his work of what has proved to be its
most effective claim on popular admiration.

But it is surely needless to point out how wofully his novels suffer as works of art from this very elementary method of procedure. As Daudet has never conceived his characters as a harmonious whole, with their external visible actions as the inevitable outcome of hidden spiritual influences, so he has found it impossible to maintain a due harmony in their conduct at such times as he presents them before the reader. We ask ourselves why Le Nabab should allow himself to be so easily befooled by the financiers of the Caisse Territoriale when he had made an immense fortune mainly by his own courage and cunning, or why little patient Désirée Delobelle after years of self-sacrificing toil should make a foolish attempt to drown herself. We should like to understand why the stolid hard-headed Astier Réhu, after facing with fortitude his public exposure before the Academy, should have felt impelled to commit suicide owing to the venomous attack made upon him in private by his wife, with whom for years he had lived in virtual estrangement; or why Queen Frédérique, so dignified in her downfall, should suddenly have forgotten herself so far as to strike her husband's valet in the face. I do not suggest that these evident inconsistencies are contrary to all human possibility—our daily life is made up of inconsistencies—but surely in a novel the hidden causes contributing to the unexpected should at least be indicated. Daudet leaves it to the reader to supply the missing links at his discretion.

Alphonse Daudet's writings divide themselves naturally into two categories: in the first we have the Provençal and autobiographical series, consisting of the majority of his short stories, *Jack*, *Le Petit Chose*, and the *Tartarin* volumes; and in the second the *mœurs Parisiennes*, starting with *Fromont Jeune et Risler Aîné*, and passing through *Le Nabab*, *Les Rois en Exil*, *Numa Roumestan*, and *Sapho*, up to *L'Immortel*. I should like to prophesy that if Daudet be read at all in the future, it will be for the sake of the earlier Provençal stories, and not for the novels on Parisian life by which mainly he made his fortune. In Provence he was at home; his natural gifts had full play; the very *mistral* had an invigorating effect upon him. To the end of his life he turned lovingly to 'notre beau Midi où l'on chante, où l'on danse, le Midi du vent, du soleil, du mirage, de tout ce qui poétise et élargit la vie.' And as a young man, as often as it was possible, he would tear himself away from Paris, and revel for a few weeks in the society of Mistral, and the little band of Provençal poets who surrounded him. At such times he was like a Highlander treading once again his native heather, and everything he wrote in the mental exhilaration produced by a sense of his native air still fresh upon him seems to me to possess an infectious gaiety not to be found in his other works. It is only in his *Contes*, first published in the *Figaro*, and subsequently collected under the titles of *Lettres de mon Moulin*, *Femmes d'Artistes*, *Contes du Lundi*, etc., that the real unspoilt Daudet is to be found. One asks oneself in despair how the author of such charming trifles as *La Mule du Pape* or *Le Roman du Chaperon Rouge* could ever have forced himself to write with infinite drudgery *Les Rois en Exil* or *Le Nabab*. Daudet, as much as any of his contemporaries, set the fashion for the short story, and within their slender limits these early fruits of his boyish fancy are perfect in form. Full of an exquisite sensibility, a quaintness of conception, their greatest charm is still their absolute spontaneousness. They are the facile creation of a gay and sympathetic imagination, constructed from the slightest materials. Sometimes there is no pretence at a story or incident, the author simply paints a picture which stands out in luminous colours, as in *Les Vieux*, a glimpse of an old married couple waited on by two little orphans in blue; or in *Les Deux Auberges*, the one silent and deserted, the other crowded and noisy. Occasionally he may be trivial, but he is never banal, never commonplace, and the little stories seem to retain a perennial freshness of sentiment.

In the later *Contes* the imagination is less vagrant, and the author has drawn more freely upon his personal experiences. Many of his stories deal with Algiers, where Daudet spent a winter for the sake of his health, and where his passion for Southern colouring received a strong impetus, and many are suggested by the events of the Franco-German War. Even here the quaintly humorous note is not altogether wanting, as in the frivolous little tale of *Les Petits Pâtés*, carried all the way to Versailles on a day of insurrection ; but the stories, written as they were for a daily paper, come to reflect more and more the melancholy feelings of the time. Daudet had already learned the value of pathos in fiction. *Le Petit Chose* triumphed by its tears ; and even to-day, in spite of its morbid sentimentality and the obvious amateurishness in the treatment—it was the first long book on which Daudet had embarked—it is still possible to read with pleasure all the early chapters, the *naïve* recital of the woes that befell the poor little poet as *pion* in a French college. There is a growing tendency to dwell on the sad and ignoble side of human life, yet, happily, he can never see life wholly *en noir*. Take the little sketch of *Arthur*, the drunken husband who squanders his money and beats his wife on Saturday nights. Zola and his imitators would have seen nothing beyond the brutal fact, and would have depicted wife and children permanently *abrutis* by hunger and ill-treatment. Daudet, on the contrary, realised that to even the most squalid home there come moments of peace and relaxation; and so he adds a half-comic, half-pathetic scene of the drunkard on Sunday afternoon singing sentimental songs on the balcony for the entertainment of admiring neighbours and his relenting wife. It seems to me a characteristic example of his attitude towards his art.

Daudet's friendship with Zola, and his temporary adhesion to the principles inculcated by the Médan school, exercised the most fatal results on his artistic career. Endowed by nature with a charming talent for improvising graceful fancies, the novelist came to persuade himself that his vocation in art lay in the laborious reproduction of life in its most material features. And so he launched into his long series of *mœurs Parisiennes*, in each of which a certain phase of Parisian life, the one more repulsive than the other, is elaborately and scrupulously portrayed. In his later life there was nothing he was more proud of than his endless notebooks—the bricks and mortar with which his literary palaces were to be built. It became a mania with him to accumulate descriptions, thoughts, anecdotes, names, with a view to future production. It was his boast that his characters were all taken from life, and were studied *sur le vif*, and were in no sense the creation of his own imagination. It is difficult to conceive of a more lamentable misconception. Daudet deliberately did his utmost to smother his natural optimistic temperament beneath the dead weight of realistic pessimism. He crowded his pages with rogues and vagabonds, with fortune-hunters and *intrigantes*. The hideous corruption lying close behind a brilliant civilisation, the secret vices of the great, the unblushing rapacity of the poor, the effrontery of all in the ruthless struggle for wealth and power, became to him absorbing subjects of study. It is in *Le Nabab*, and its immediate successor, *Les Rois en Exil*, that the evil effects of this unfortunate development are to be seen in their most destructive form. Even at the time, the success of these volumes was mainly a *succès de scandale*, and to-day it is difficult to conceive of any one reading them for pleasure. Properly speaking, neither is a novel at all; neither has any unity of interest or of action. They are chapters, *bien documentés*, of Parisian social history of the day. Each consists of a series of descriptive passages, of pictures crowded with characters and overladen with detail, of incidents strung together by the very slightest connecting thread.

In Turgenev's published correspondence there is a remark referring to the publication of *Le Nabab*. 'I think,' the Russian novelist writes to a friend, 'I shall make up my mind to write him a *truthful* letter.' And then, on second thoughts, remembering how sensitive his brother-novelist was to adverse criticism, he adds: 'Perhaps, after all, I shall do nothing of the kind.' It is not difficult to imagine the line of criticism that the creator of 'Lisa' would have adopted towards his friend, whom he so clearly saw to be launched on a disastrous track. I am fully aware that there are pages of description in these volumes which have called forth the enthusiastic admiration of distinguished French critics by their conscientious exactitude, their convincing truth. Daudet has been at great pains to hunt up curious and little-known developments of Paris life, such as the Agence Tom Lévis, the house in which Élysée Méraut had lived for eighteen years, the church of the Franciscan fathers, and has painted them with elaborate and even startling *vraisemblance*. But these lengthy descriptions have, as a rule, the very slenderest connection with the main story, and by their number and prolixity they become intolerably wearisome.

Their very vividness and accuracy are productive of a sense of disproportion; as much emphasis is given to the most insignificant detail as to the central figure. Everything is placed in the forefront of the picture, in the full glare of the light. There is no appreciation of values, no fading away into the distance, no gradation of tone. In the end the rapid succession of one impression after another fatigues the eye, as it is fatigued by a revolving kaleidoscope. And when all is said, the fundamental question arises, whether the subject has been the least worthy of treatment. The private vices of dethroned monarchs, the mass of avarice and corruption that seethes round the successful parvenu—why need we pry into one or the other? They have no real bearing on the problems of human life. They do not touch any of the fundamental chords of the human heart. At best they are but the accidental and abnormal product of an artificial society. Even *Sapho*, with all its faults, can claim a far stronger justification for its existence. In it, Daudet describes a certain phase in the relations between man and woman which must have had its counterpart in every age. But for the two volumes we have been examining, it is difficult to find any justification. The characters are almost uniformly sordid and despicable; it is only here and there—in the affection of Le Nabab for his aged mother, or in the relations of Queen Frédérique to her afflicted little son—that we can gain a glimpse of the Daudet who wrote *Lettres de mon Moulin*. Over all the rest, the curse of so-called realism lies heavily.

It is pleasant to remember that this was only a phase in the novelist's career. A great deal of the evil influence had been flung off a couple of years later, when Daudet published *Numa Roumestan*. Here he is back again in his natural element; for the book, though nominally belonging to the *mœurs Parisiennes* series, deals almost exclusively with his beloved Midi. And of all Daudet's more ambitious efforts, it is in my opinion the only novel that can still be read with any real enjoyment. In a sense *Numa* is the complement to *Tartarin*; the one is the caricature, the other the reality. Of Tartarin, what can be said that has not been said a hundred times? It was written in the exuberance of the novelist's youth, but it appeals to men of every age. It has been the source of genuine merriment to hundreds of thousands of readers. For myself, I must confess that literary caricature has as a rule no attraction, and *Tartarin sur les Alpes* I have never been able to accomplish. But the *Aventures Prodigieuses*, in spite of a strong previous prejudice against it, vanquished me by its irresistible verve, and by the delightful air of conviction which invests the absurd story with all the importance of a historical narrative. The broad farce is relieved by many touches of delicate irony, and by charming first impressions of the semi-tropical Algerian scenery, which made so vivid an impression on the young traveller. Like a true Provençal, Daudet is himself carried away by the irresistible tendency of his brain towards exaggeration. As the story advances he trades more and more recklessly on the gullibility of his readers, piling up marvel upon marvel, until at length the culminating point is reached, when the irrepressible camel pursues the train that conveys the hero from Marseilles home to Tarascon, and shares in the welcome at the station. 'Une noble bête,' says Tartarin calmly. 'Elle m'a vu tuer tous mes lions.'

Having thus delivered his soul over *Tartarin*, Daudet was able to paint a real sober picture of the Meridional in *Numa Roumestan*. 'L'Homme du Midi,' he remarks in the *Aventures Prodigieuses*, 'ne ment pas, il se trompe. Il ne dit pas toujours la vérité, mais il croit la dire. Son mensonge à lui ce n'est pas du mensonge, c'est une espèce de mirage.' *Numa Roumestan* seems to have been written in illustration of the aphorism, and certainly Daudet has never come so close to real character-drawing as in his description of the 'grand Méridional,' his talents and his weaknesses, his easy good-nature, his colossal egotism, his utter untrustworthiness. He has a thorough grip of his subject, and he enters into it with all the zest of his earlier manner. For many years Numa was accepted as a kindly caricature of Gambetta. In reality Daudet was deliberately painting an unkind portrait of himself with his little weaknesses enlarged into vices, and his own marriage, which was so conspicuous a success, turned to failure. For there can be no doubt that Rosalie, with her serious well-balanced northern temperament and her admirable virtues, is none other than Mme. Daudet, who kept a restraining hand on her husband's prodigalities, and changed the gay casual bohemian into the hard-working *père de famille*. It is no doubt because the story of Numa came home to him so closely that he has been able to invest it with a human interest far above that of his other books. The problem of the fusion of North and South, which lies at the root of so many of the apparent inconsistencies in the French character, was strongly exemplified in his own household, and to the novelist it naturally suggested much interesting speculation. Mme. Daudet was a woman of unusual culture, and herself a critic to whose judgment her husband constantly referred. That his marriage was a singularly happy one is the testimony of all their friends. But it seems to me a question whether the life of a prosperous *bourgeois* which, thanks in a great measure to his wife's admirable supervision, the novelist was enabled to lead, served the higher interests of his art, whether it might not have prospered better in a garret of the Quartier Latin, or better still, in some Provençal village, and whether all the circumstances of his marriage did not interpose a barrier between him and that Provençal life from which he drew all his best inspiration. The tendency of the *milieu* in which his later life was spent was to place the novelist's work on too high a plane and to urge him into methods of composition quite foreign to his natural bent, with the inevitable result of a great loss in spontaneity and grace, his two most valuable qualities. And in this tendency

I cannot but feel that Mme. Daudet had her share of responsibility. Something of all this may have lain at the back of the novelist's mind when after twenty years of married life he wrote his *Numa Roumestan*, holding the balance as between man and wife with a scrupulous care throughout the story. Yet it is clear that at heart the sympathies of the author are all with his florid hero; and his ill-doings, if unsparingly chronicled, are treated with a lightness of touch which is in thorough keeping with the theme. The episode of the '*tambourinaire*' and Hortense's foolish devotion to Valmajour are somewhat in the *Tartarin* spirit; but in his very best manner are the pages describing the Provençal warehouse in Paris 'aux produits du Midi,' where the *patois*, the noise, the disorder recalled the South, and where all the Méridionaux of the quarter forgathered, feeling themselves at home 'un peu comme en foire de Beaucaire.' Through the elaborate and rapturous enumeration of the goods, from the green olives to the celebrated *brandade de morue*, piled on the shelves of the Mèfre establishment, one feels that nostalgia for the South which caused Daudet to take an intense delight in this little oasis of popular Provençal life dropped down in the arid desert of Parisian boulevards.

During the last ten or twelve years of his life Daudet wrote little. The chronic pain of an incurable disease which rendered all exertion irksome explains this decline in literary activity. But his name was kept prominently before the public by the great controversy concerning his attitude towards the Academy, a controversy the echoes of which lingered around his deathbed. To Englishmen the quarrel savours somewhat of a storm in a teacup, but for the average Frenchman, before whose eyes the Academy looms in majestic proportions, the publication of *L'Immortel* became an event of almost national importance. Whether Daudet's attitude was the result of mere petulant caprice or of definite conviction, he certainly allowed his natural *bonhomie* to forsake him when he held up to grotesque ridicule the petty weaknesses of forty estimable citizens. *L'Immortel* is written throughout in a very *méchant* mood; and apart from the special circumstances of its production, it has already become very tedious reading. The prejudice is too bitter, the sarcasm too unmeasured, and the whole assumption on which the main attack is based—*i.e.* the possibility of a scholar in Astier Réhu's position being the dupe of a whole series of historical forgeries—is in the highest degree improbable. From the literary standpoint *L'Immortel* is a failure, as novels with too obvious a purpose are apt to be. But in the end it is probable that Daudet's reputation was enhanced by his revolt against national conventionality; for the Academy could have given him nothing that he did not already enjoy, and his refusal to seat himself among the Immortals adorned him, in the eyes at least of foreigners, with a halo of disinterestedness, not, I fear, altogether merited.

A year or two before his death Daudet broke silence with *La Petite Paroisse*. It was almost like listening to the voice of some previous generation, and the book was received with a certain reverent curiosity. It cannot be said to have added to the author's reputation. The story is long, rather confused, deficient in clearness of outline. Yet it is interesting as indicating a definite rupture with the naturalist school, accompanied by a widened appreciation of human life, a more charitable interpretation of human motive. Lydie Fénigan, the heroine, is an attempt at a psychological study—not very successful in its results, for it is equally difficult to understand why she eloped with the little prince, and why she came back to her husband. That the attempt should have been made seems to show that *malgré lui* Daudet had become infected with some of the new literary ideals that had grown up around him. And the book indicates further an acquiescence, if nothing more, in that revival of religious belief which, in one form or another, has been one of the distinctive notes of French literature during the last few years. The instinctive optimism of his youth had crystallised into a benevolent philosophy of life, and a merely superficial agnosticism had fallen away before a dawning sense of the mystery of life.

The glamour with which Daudet was invested at the time of his death has faded away, and it is possible to arrive at a due estimate of his permanent place in literature. We cannot honestly persuade ourselves that it will be a high one. Yet it is impossible to arrive at the conviction without a feeling of sadness and regret. Daudet was brilliantly successful; he was one of the most popular novelists of his day; he made a large fortune; he could afford at the last to despise the Academy. For the majority of men such a career means everything that the world can give; for others it is perfectly compatible with failure—failure in all that makes for permanent fame. And it is just here that Daudet has failed. I cannot rid myself of the impression that he ought to have written far better books than he did, something at least, apart from *Tartarin de Tarascon*, which might have survived into the coming century. But he never penetrated beyond the trivialities of life. And it is more than probable that the higher estimate of his natural powers is based on a misconception, and the sense of disappointment may merely be due to the fact that the judgment of maturer years cannot endorse the uncritical admiration of youth. It is always baffling to be brought face to face with the objects of an early veneration.

J. K. HUYSMANS

In the history of a human soul there are times of stress and times of lull; there are days of fiery combat followed by long months of seeming inertia and spiritual torpor. It was of the former that M. Huysmans wrote in *En Route*, perhaps the most extraordinary book of recent years. In *La Cathédrale* he has led his pilgrim Durtal by slow and deliberate steps through the intermediate stage that divides his repentance at La Trappe from his entrance into the Benedictine monastery of Solesmes. It is a period of introspection and orientation, of patient self-communing and silent longing, a period that must come to every soul if the work of conversion and illumination is to be a permanent one. Its interest is purely subjective; there is no action, no incident, hardly any characterisation. It belongs to M. Huysmans alone to create a novel from such a lack of external circumstance. I doubt whether any other living writer would have ventured on so apparently thankless a task. Of necessity the dramatic element which played so large a part in *En Route* is entirely absent from its sequel. The great fight between faith and unfaith is over ; and as far as the outside world is concerned, the curtain might well have been rung down on the victor. But to Huysmans as to Maeterlinck, and indeed to all whose gaze would penetrate beneath life's surface, the real tragedy of our existence only begins there where external adventures and dangers cease, and the silent hidden life of the dreamer and the mystic possesses a charm and a value denied to that of the man of action.

For my own part, I am filled with a sense of gratitude towards M. Huysmans for having given us *La Cathédrale*. It is full of beautiful writing, of wonderful descriptive pages, of delicate appreciations, of spiritual insight into Christian symbolism. It opens up unsuspected vistas of thought, and invests even familiar objects with a new and profound significance. For lovers of religious and Catholic art, for students of architecture, for all whose souls have been touched however lightly by the remote beauty of mysticism, almost every page will appear endowed with a gentle deliberate charm. Yet it is difficult to believe that the book will ever enjoy a wide popularity with the general English public. Its very form as fiction will tell against it. Rightly or wrongly, the average novel-reader does expect a certain play of incident, a pretence at least at plot, and in *La Cathédrale* he will find neither. Even the incomparable Mme. Bavoil, through whose intervention the reader in the early chapters looks for some relaxation from the strenuous purpose of the author, is kept sternly in the domestic background of the Abbé Gévresin's lodging. Anticipating amusement, I can conceive that he will pronounce many of Huysmans' most beautiful pages intolerably tedious. And it must be admitted that these are often strung together with a clumsiness which it is surprising to find in a literary artist of M. Huysmans' experience. His transitions are carelessly effected, and the little incidents that seemingly *malgré lui* he is forced to introduce serve merely as so many pegs on which to hang his erudite disquisitions. With an over-prodigal hand he pours out before the reader his treasures of mediæval lore, the strange medley of learning that he has acquired by long gleaning in the by-paths of the world's history. It would be easy to prove that M. Huysmans might have constructed a more effective book from out of the vast storehouse of his knowledge. But even in the somewhat disjointed state in which he has elected to give his work to the world, there are treasures of thought, of description, of learning which silence criticism.

No writer can equal M. Huysmans in sheer descriptive power. Flaubert produced an incomparable effect by his deliberate detailed pictures, his unrivalled skill in the choice of an appropriate adjective. Zola merely sees the obvious and superficial, and enumerates his points like the items in a catalogue. But Huysmans seizes at once the spiritual and the material; he identifies himself with his subject, he breathes its atmosphere, and not a detail of the physical features escapes him. Perhaps it was a sub-conscious knowledge of his own power that led him to Chartres, where he found in the Cathedral a subject worthy of his pen. It is to Chartres that he conveys his hero in company with the Abbé Gévresin, and throughout the book the Cathedral—its history, its architecture, its symbolism—is intimately interwoven with Durtal's soul's progress. Thanks to M. Huysmans, Chartres will henceforth live in our imaginations as it has never lived before. To bring a great work of art within the understanding of the multitude, to make it a living reality to those whose eyes have never been gladdened by its vision, is surely a creative act second only to that of the original creators. With an ecstasy born of faith, the author has steeped himself in the atmosphere of the sacred pile. To him it is a poem in stone, a sublime prayer come down to us from the Middle Ages, a living monument to the faith of the past. He hurries thither at early dawn in order to see the morning light steal through the forest of slender pillars, and he spends long hours in solitary contemplation of its marvellous sculptured porches. He singles out its beauties one by one—its statues, its stone traceries, the tender vivid blue of its incomparable windows —and he describes each detail with the elaborate precision that he acquired from his early training in the naturalist school. But permeating all he discerns the mystery of faith, the presence of the unseen, the mystic influence of the Blessed Virgin to whose worship the Cathedral is dedicated. No saint shares in her honours; no hallowed bones rest beneath the pavement of her temple; to Mary alone, to the two miraculous Madonnas of Notre-Dame de Sous-Terre, and Notre-Dame du Pilier, her suppliant worshippers turn for consolation. Among these Durtal comes to be numbered; with Verlaine he registers the vow, 'Je ne veux plus aimer que ma mère Marie'; and devotion to the Virgin—who in the religion of the pious Frenchman occupies much the same place as his own mother fills in his family affections— becomes inextricably mingled with his æsthetic reveries on line and colour.

Gothic architecture to Huysmans is the purest, noblest expression in stone of man's aspirations towards the divine. Its pointed archways, its tall, slender spires spring heavenward like tender, confident, audacious prayers.

'Romanesque,' he writes, 'is the La Trappe of architecture; it gives shelter to austere Orders, to sombre convents, to men who kneel on ashes chanting penitential psalms in plaintive voices, with heads bowed low. . . . From its Asiatic origin Romanesque has retained something of the pre-Christian era; within its walls man prays to the implacable Adonaï rather than to the charitable Child, the tender Mother. Gothic architecture, on the other hand, is less timid, more concerned with the Second and Third Persons of the Trinity and with the Virgin; it shelters Orders that are less rigorous and more artistic; beneath its roof prostrate figures rise up, lowered eyes are raised, and sepulchral voices grow seraphic.'

In a word, Romanesque for Huysmans typifies the Old Testament, and Gothic the New. And of all the marvellous Gothic cathedrals dotted over France, the Cathedral of Chartres, 'une blonde aux yeux bleus,' appeals to him as the most devotional, the most etherealised in its beauty. After long pages of 'architectural exegesis,' he sums up his impressions of the lofty interior in an outburst of rapturous devotion—

'Elle se spiritualisait, se faisait toute âme toute prière, lorsqu'elle s'élançait vers le Seigneur pour le rejoindre ; légère et gracile, presque impondérable, elle était l'expression la plus magnifique de la beauté qui s'évade de sa gangue terrestre, de la beauté qui se séraphise. Elle était grêle et pâle comme ces Vierges de Roger van der Weyden qui sont si filiformes, si fluettes, qu'elles s'envoleraient si elles n'étaient en quelque sorte retenues ici-bas par le poids de leurs brocarts et de leurs traînes.'

Many will be tempted to read *La Cathédrale* solely for the sake of the beautiful descriptive passages which abound in its pages. And from that point of view alone the book is infinitely worth reading. And yet the descriptions of Chartres are subsidiary in intention to the description of Durtal's state of soul, and the great moral purpose of the book is of higher import than its æsthetic qualities. In its spiritual aspect, if not in all its material details, *La Cathédrale* is a chapter in an autobiography as truthful and as penetrating as any of the great confessions which remain for all time among the most fascinating and instructive of human documents. No one in discussing, let us say, the *Confessions of St. Augustine*, would restrict himself solely to the literary aspect of the work, and to do so in the case of Huysmans would be not less ineffectual. *Là Bas*, *En Route*, and *La Cathédrale* form the veracious history of a soul's conversion from materialism of the grossest kind to faith of a high spiritual order. And the story has been told by one of the greatest literary artists of the day. It is here that its almost unique value becomes evident. In it we are brought face to face with the essential truths of life presented in their most convincing aspect. If, as it is sometimes alleged, genius is neither more nor less than a capacity for perfect honesty of thought and expression, the writers of great autobiography —their names can be counted on the fingers of one hand—cannot fall short of genius. For to be honest about oneself is of all gifts the most rare. Even Cellini's candid and fascinating *Vita* is written with a touch of bravado, and the *Mémoires* of Jean Jacques Rousseau have more than a touch of assumed sentimentalism. St. Augustine shares perhaps with St. Teresa the palm of supreme excellence in the sphere of spiritual revelations. Both were giants of the intellectual as well as of the spiritual life. Many of the mystical saints have manifested their interior life as an act of obedience and humility, but only a few possessed, in addition to purity of intention, those gifts of mind without which the gifts of the spirit cannot be made intelligible to the outside world. In J. K. Huysmans the necessary qualities are combined in a singularly high degree. He possesses an amazing, and to me an incomprehensible, capacity for squandering his soul on paper, for gauging the idiosyncrasies of his own temperament, for seizing his most fugitive emotions and pigeon-holing them for future literary use. That, in his three autobiographical volumes, he should have screened his identity behind the convenient mask of fiction, does not detract in any way from the sincerity of his work. Nowhere has he attempted to build up a personalty around the figure of Durtal, to create a character for him by the aid of artistic embellishments. From first to last he writes of himself, from his own point of view, and the sense of his identity with his hero is so strong, that we might almost believe the personal pronoun had been replaced by the fictitious name only on the eve of publication.

Many readers of *En Route* declared themselves sceptical as to the reality of the author's reconciliation with the Catholic Church, of which the book professes to be the record. They maintained that the religious attitude was a mere pose adopted for artistic effect. The extraordinarily dramatic treatment of purely spiritual experiences afforded perhaps some superficial excuse for so fundamentally false a view. I do not think that any reader could fall into the same error after reading *La Cathédrale*. Faith — vivid, unquestioning, mediæval—is stamped on every page. It is full from beginning to end of that sense of finality that comes to the human soul after a long wrestle with the withering torments of unbelief. It is altogether more humane, more charitable than its predecessor, less prolific in bitter sarcasm and rash judgments against all who fall short of the spiritual ideals of the neophyte. The patient study of which the book gives evidence—it is the outcome of three years' labour—could only have been voluntarily undertaken by one drawn irresistibly to such subjects by the magnetism of faith. Huysmans' soul is one that could never have accommodated itself to a purely negative creed. Religion alone could save him from incurable melancholy. All his life he has suffered from a veritable craving after the supernatural and a crushing sense of the misery of our material existence. In his most unbelieving period, with that curious perversity of the intellect which frequently prompts men to cling to the most petty superstitions after they have thrown off all so-called 'orthodox' belief, he flung himself for a time into the study of Satanism, Magic, and those varied spiritualistic phenomena from which a jaded Parisian public seeks to gain some new excitement, hoping to find relief from the intolerable tedium of his days. The very excesses of his sensual life can be explained as a blind striving after the unattainable. Then grace came to him, and he turned once more to the Catholic faith of his childhood. Of the struggle that ensued between the spirit and the flesh the most elaborate and convincing picture is drawn in *En Route*. All convention, all reticence is cast aside, and the naked soul of the sinner is exhibited in a hand-to-hand struggle with the forces of evil that his own vicious life has drawn upon him. The recital fills one with a sense of awe, of the grandeur of life's combat, such a sense as comes to one before the Last Judgment in the Sistine. And over all there is the conviction, subtly conveyed, that of himself, Durtal, timid, hesitating, even reluctant, could have effected nothing; that he would have been helpless before the torrent of temptations that assailed him had he not been borne forward by some irresistible force, some compelling power, the 'yet not I' of the apostle. For, in truth, Durtal himself is a sorry hero, who enlists our sympathies only by the candour and humility of his miserable revelations. True, there is in him no touch of self-glorification, none of the morbid vanity of the reformed drunkard 'testifying' to the excesses of his unregenerate state.

But even in *La Cathédrale*, when he has fought the great fight and has reached a haven of comparative calm and security, he is at best plodding, conscientious, humble, but never heroic. There is a want of robustness about him which, I confess, fills me at times with an unreasonable irritation. For, in reality, Durtal is an accurate study of human nature painted with the patient fidelity of Van Eyck; and his very frailty brings into prominent relief the doctrine of sanctification by grace, which is the underlying 'motif' of the whole autobiography.

From his first revolt against materialism it is Christianity in its most mystical aspect that has attracted Durtal. He spurns the utilitarianism that has crept into much of the so-called Christianity of the present day. He is even bitterly and uncharitably intolerant of prim piety, of the worldly compromises of a 'bourgeoisie dévote,' of religious observances performed in a narrow and Pharisaic spirit. His soul yearns after the highest life, the fullest comprehension of the Infinite. He is not a mystic, but he is a keen-sighted and sympathetic student of mysticism. He has made a prolonged and critical study of the mystical writings of the Middle Ages, of St. Bernard and St. John of the Cross, of St. Gertrude and St. Angela, and of his own mediæval countryman the Admirable Ruysbroeck, from whom Maeterlinck also has drawn many of the purest thoughts in *Le Trésor des Humbles*. The lives of the mystical saints appeal to him intensely, and he paints them with a passion of sympathy which brings out at once their spiritual grandeur and their touching human weakness. I look forward eagerly to that life of Blessed Lidwine which he has repeatedly foreshadowed. Indeed, I would like a whole series of lives of saints from his pen. They would be full of supernatural grace and passionate human feeling, far indeed removed from the edifying lay-figure of the conventional hagiographer, for whom he has so profound a contempt. Take his little sketch of the almost unknown Dutch Carmelite of the seventeenth century, Marie Marguerite des Anges, whose life of amazing mortification was crowned after death by a miracle. She appears before us as real, as true, as palpable in Huysmans' few ecstatic pages as if her life had been passed on our own plane of daily existence, instead of in a spiritual atmosphere of which most of us can form simply no conception at all. To Huysmans the contemplative life is the highest good, the most complete realisation of the end for which man is created. For him, as for the mystic, the spiritual life alone is real, and present, and actual; the material life, that which we realise by our senses, is dim and temporary and of no account. Monasticism, the life of the cloister, where alone the contemplative life can flourish, hovers unceasingly before his vision as the ultimate goal. Both his latest books are penetrated by the sense of its beauty, of its extraordinary fascination. He brings it before the reader in a way that no great novelist has done before, that no English novelist has ever attempted. Here, in modern industrial England we have entirely lost sight of the spiritual value of the ascetic life—and a life of contemplation is of necessity founded on the rock-bed of asceticism—oblivious that the greatest wisdom and the purest knowledge have come down to us through no other channel. We are apt to talk of monasticism as though it were some exploded fallacy of a superstitious past instead of its being the natural expression of one of the most profound and permanent cravings of human nature. We see the external triviality, the superficial narrowness of the religious life, and we entirely fail to see its hidden significance, the great underlying truths of which the material acts are but the outward expression. The life of the soldier in its daily round of drill and guard-duty and rigid discipline would appear equally petty and futile, were it not within the comprehension of us all that it constitutes an essential preparation for deeds of heroism on the battle-field. So the daily life of the monk or nun, the prayer, the silence, the mortifications are an essential preparation for that more intimate union with the Divine which is of the essence of all mysticism. And to the true soldier, as to the true religious, the imposed privations and the daily discipline are joyfully borne as the appointed means towards a supreme end.

To Huysmans alone among modern novelists

there has come this unique comprehension of all that is concealed behind the wall of the cloister. He is as keenly alive to the refined spirituality that distinguishes communities of women as to the more robust virtues of the male Orders. Nor is his admiration based upon a romantic and imaginary conception of cloistered life. His fundamental realism does not fail him even here. He notes the coarse chapped hands and plain freckled faces of some humble Franciscan Sisters, in whose chapel he has gone to pray, and at La Trappe there is no attempt to gloss over the repulsive physical details inseparable from a life of extreme toil and mortification. If in his picture of 'le frère Siméon,' the strongest and the most astounding thing he has ever accomplished, he has ventured for an instant to lift the veil that shrouds the regions of spiritual ecstasy from the eyes of an unbelieving generation, he has none the less noted with an almost savage fidelity the unsavoury surroundings of the swineherd's daily life. It is the essential beauty of a life of prayer and renunciation that appeals to him. He has steeped himself in the sentiment of the

Middle Ages; he has familiarised himself with the most ecstatic revelations of conventual visionaries until the veiled arcana of the religious life stand revealed before him. It is only possible to mention the description of Notre Dame de l'Atre in *En Route*, for it would be impossible to speak in adequate terms of pages so eloquent, so intimate, so filled with spiritual enlightenment. In *La Cathédrale* the penitential ideal of Trappist austerity has given place to the gentler, more cultivated, ideal of Benedictine learning. It is the Benedictines who have preserved for us the glorious traditions of plain-chant; it is in their convents and monasteries alone that the Divine Office is rendered with all the solemnity, all the measured beauty of which it is capable. The incomparable liturgy of the Church is the subject of their constant solicitude. They have been the zealous guardians of religious art in music, in painting, in architecture; and they have declined to countenance the *singeries musicales* and tawdry decoration which an irreligious age has introduced into the Sanctuary. To Durtal, a student and a recluse, whose æsthetic tastes are inextricably mingled with his religious aspirations, the Order of St. Benedict presents features of irresistible attractiveness. As he says of himself in *La Cathédrale*: 'He had nothing else in his favour, but at least he could plead a passionate love of mysticism and of the liturgy, of plain-chant and of cathedrals! Truthfully, and without self-deception, he could say, "Lord, I have loved the beauty of Thy house and the place where Thy glory dwelleth."' In a Benedictine monastery, if anywhere, he may find peace for his tortured soul, and a rule of life not too austere for his poor shattered body. Slowly he feels himself drawn, as by invisible cords, until in the closing pages of his book he stands on the threshold of Solesmes. *L'Oblat* is already announced, but it probably will not be given to the world until M. Huysmans has definitely severed himself from his Parisian life. Personally, I hope it may be so; for a study of monastic life in the present day, written with an inside knowledge, not, as is usually the case, by some renegade monk, but by one gifted with all the spiritual and artistic qualifications for such a task, would certainly prove a document of the highest human interest. It may be reserved for M. Huysmans to carry forward with his pen that revival of monasticism in France which Lacordaire, preaching to all Paris from the pulpit of Notre Dame in the proscribed white robes of the Dominican, initiated by his penetrating eloquence and the magnetism of his personal example.

The conversion of M. Huysmans is no isolated episode in the history of contemporary French literature. Whether or no it heralds, as many have assumed, the dawn of a Christian renaissance in France, it may unquestionably be held to indicate a revolt against materialism, both in faith and in literature. Verlaine and Huysmans, Ferdinand Brunetière and François Coppée have each in turn, and according to the measure of his abilities, borne witness to one and the same truth. They have, one and all, deliberately altered their attitude towards life, and have publicly burned the gods whom they previously adored. Naturalism in art and materialism in religion have outlived their day in Paris, and the swing of the pendulum is now set in the contrary direction. Men have wearied of mere exteriority, of faithful photographic reproduction, and they have wearied above all of the attitude of mind which can only perceive the sordid and repulsive side of life. Amid the strange tangle of vague religious aspirations and fantastic spiritualistic beliefs with which all classes in Paris seem to be infected at the present time, we can discern a real craving after the invisible, a longing for closer union with the spiritual forces of existence. It is on these lines alone that we can hope for the revival of literature from the present condition of national decadence. Literature is in the main true to life just in so far as it marks the eternal correspondence between the seen and the unseen; and to-day we are learning to realise afresh the value of symbolism as a means of bringing home this correspondence to the world's intelligence. In France it seems to me at least possible that this revolt against materialism may crystallise into a definite revival of Catholic faith. French literature has always represented within its boundaries the two extremes of a licentious paganism and the expression of an intense Christian spirituality.

The literary level of purely devotional writing has usually been very much higher in France than in other countries, Spain alone, perhaps, excepted. The pagan and the Christian element in literature dominate each other in turn in succeeding waves of national emotion. In the earlier years of the present century there occurred an unexpected recrudescence of Christian faith when Chateaubriand gave the signal with his *Génie du Christianisme*, and De Maistre and Lamartine, Lamennais and Montalembert devoted their pens with a passionate energy to the service of the Church. To-day, under altered conditions, and on a somewhat wider basis, the same phenomenon may repeat itself; and the symbolist movement, with the author of *En Route* as its most penetrating exponent, may mark the advent of a new period of spiritual efflorescence on Gallic soil.

To the critic M. Huysmans' art presents many conflicting qualities. We shall understand it better if we bear in mind that he is, by early training, a realist. Zola, who makes no mistakes, except in literature, always knew that Huysmans, and not Maupassant, was the man of genius.

To-day, freeing himself from the shackles of the naturalist school, he transfers to the spiritual plane all the accuracy, the conscientiousness, the powers of observation which he acquired in the past. He penetrates to the spiritual meaning of life with the same unerring precision as in former years he painted external features. There are even times when old associations are so strong upon him that he seems to take pleasure in applying ignoble words to spiritual purposes with a jarring effect. It is one of the few blots on a style at once singularly harmonious and extraordinarily terse and daring. Symbolism, that most elusive of studies, he reduces to an exact science. He has mastered it in all its details, all its ramifications. He enters exhaustively into the symbolism of numbers and of gems, of colours and scents, of beasts and birds, and he tabulates the conflicting theories of saints and of scholars. That on a subject so suggestive and so beautiful he should have ended by wearying the reader with a mass of ill-arranged detail is a matter of very real regret. He has possessed himself by much reading of a vast store of rare and somewhat fantastic information, pigeon-holed ready for use. But, like Zola, he lacks discrimination in the use of his material; he keeps nothing back, forgetful that the reader's appetite may not be as exorbitant as his own. The superficial critic will probably condemn his habit of intercalating in his narrative long pages which have no direct connection with his subject. D'Annunzio sins in the same way. It is a proceeding that violates the accepted canons of literary construction of our day. But if canons are violated with good results, where is the evil? The proceeding becomes rather an affirmation of a new law. And the long criticism of Fra Angelico in *La Cathédrale*, though at first sight it may annoy us as a digression, grows upon us by degrees, until we come to see that it lights up the book as one of the beautiful windows at Chartres lights up the dim interior.

I would like to take leave of M. Huysmans in one of his happier, more imaginative, moods. His is a dark, strenuous soul, to whom even the full light of Christian faith brings but a small share of that 'holy joy,' of which Francis of Assisi will always remain the most exquisite type. But in *La Cathédrale* we see traces of a melting pessimism, of softened judgments, of gleams of radiance penetrating the natural gloom of his soul. Here, on the eve of his departure for Solesmes, are the words in which he sums up his impressions of Chartres, the home of the Blessed Virgin, whose very features he seeks to trace in the mystic beauty of the interior :—

'Eh bien, moi, qui ne suis point un visionnaire et qui dois avoir recours à mon imagination pour me la figurer, il me semble que je l'aperçois dans les contours, dans l'expression même de la cathédrale ; les traits sont un peu brouillés dans le pâle éblouissement de la grande rose qui flamboie derrière sa tête, telle qu'un nimbe. Elle sourit et ses yeux, tout en lumière, ont l'incomparable éclat de ces clairs saphirs qui éclairent l'entrée de la nef. Son corps fluide s'effuse en une robe candide de flammes, rayée de cannelures, côtelée, ainsi que la jupe de la fausse Berthe. Son visage a une blancheur qui se nacre, et la chevelure, comme tissée par un rouet de soleil, vole en des fils d'or ; Elle est l'Épouse du Cantique : "Pulchra ut luna, electa ut sol." La basilique où Elle réside et qui se confond avec Elle s'illumine de ses grâces ; les gemmes des verrières chantent ses vertus ; les colonnes minces et frêles qui s'élancent d'un jet, des dalles jusques aux combles, décèlent ses aspirations et ses désirs ; le pavé raconte son humilité ; les voûtes qui se réunissent, de même qu'un dais, au-dessus d'Elle, narrent sa charité ; les pierres et les vitres répètent ses antiennes ; et il n'est pas jusqu'à l'aspect belliqueux de quelques détails du sanctuaire, jusqu'à cette tournure chevaleresque rappelant les Croisades, avec les lames d'épées et les boucliers des fenêtres et des roses, le casque des ogives, les cottes de maille du clocher vieux, les treillis de fer de certains carreaux, qui n'évoquent le souvenir du capitule de Prime et de l'antienne de Laudes de son petit office, qui ne traduise le " terribilis ut castrorum acies ordinata " qui ne relate cette privauté qu'Elle possède, quand Elle le veut, d'être "ainsi qu'une armée rangée en bataille, terrible."

'Mais Elle ne le veut pas souvent ici, je crois ; aussi cette cathédrale est-elle surtout le reflet de son inépuisable mansuétude, l'écho de son impartible gloire!'

We see in this beautiful passage the beneficent influence exercised by the great Gothic cathedral on the soul of the novelist. His six months at Chartres were spent in a spiritual ecstasy. Even in those moments of prostration, by which the fidelity of every soul is tested, he is conscious at Chartres of some tender spiritual protection which saves him from the lowest depths of desolation. He is lifted up out of the region of petty personal miseries which in the early pages of *En Route* were seen to paralyse his soul, and he lives in a new world—a world of dreams and aspiration and mystical beauty. There is a long spiritual pilgrimage between the Black Mass in *Là Bas* and the Communion in the crypt of Chartres. The two noblest emotions of which the soul of M. Huysmans is capable—religious faith and artistic enjoyment—find their highest expression combined within the grey walls of the Cathedral. At Chartres his soul is at peace. The book gives us a new sense of the magical force of Beauty, of the eternal power of Truth.

EMILE VERHAEREN

In a bi-lingual country literature must always suffer grave disadvantages. It lacks a national entity, and hence it fails in a measure to excite popular enthusiasm, or to achieve international recognition. Until quite recently Belgium might have been cited as a case in point. How many of us previous to the moment, some five years ago, when the fame of Maurice Maeterlinck first drifted across the North Sea, realised that the kingdom of King Leopold could lay claim to a distinctively national school of contemporary literature? Her Flemish writers were studied only by their own section of the nation, their very existence unsuspected by foreigners; her French writers, when not overshadowed by the artistic pre-eminence of her Gallic neighbour, were apt to find themselves appropriated by the latter and carelessly numbered in the ranks of her own literary sons. If to-day Belgium has openly triumphed over all these drawbacks, and if the young school of Franco-Belgian poets and dramatists has established for itself a European reputation, the fact is in itself the best possible testimony to the life and the vigour of a movement that can point to the names of Maeterlinck and Lemonnier, of Verhaeren and Rodenbach on its roll of members.

Had the brilliant group of young writers who for the last fifteen years have found their chief rallying-ground in the pages of *L'Art Moderne* resided, not in Brussels, but in Paris, it is certain that their fame would have spread far more rapidly than has been the case. They have represented 'Young Belgium' not only with spirit and talent, but even with genius; they have led the van of a movement against meaningless conventionalities and Academic precision both in prose and poetry; they have allied themselves with enthusiasm with *Les Jeunes* of the French capital; they were the defenders of the Impressionists in Art years before Impressionism had been adopted as the shibboleth of the cultured, while in their own country identifying themselves with the rising talent of Fernand Knopff, of Henry de Greux, and of Van Rysselberghe; and they have themselves in literature earned in turn the epithets of 'parnassien' and 'symbolist,' and doubtless, too, of decadent. Like the vanguard of every movement, whether political, literary, or scientific, they have had desperate rivalries and bitter enmities; quondam friends have quarrelled, old alliances have been broken, and organs have succeeded one another with bewildering rapidity—*La Jeune Belgique, La Wallonie, La Société Nouvelle, La Basoche, L'Art Jeune*—as each seceding faction has felt the need of a representative mouthpiece. Such episodes are the natural accompaniments of any young, free, and spontaneous movement, liberating itself from clogging shackles, and falling into inevitable extravagances in the process of finding its own feet and realising its own necessary limitations. And even the extravagances should be welcomed with a sympathetic indulgence if we would arrive at an understanding of the true inwardness of a movement of which they are but the accidental exteriorities.

From its first inception the name of Émile Verhaeren, so familiar in Brussels and in Paris, so little known comparatively on this side of the Channel, has been intimately associated with what we may call the new Belgian literary school. For many years he has been accepted as one of its most brilliant leaders. As a student at Louvain towards the year 1880, Verhaeren founded, in conjunction with his friend and present publisher, E. Deman, a militant little sheet, *La Semaine*, which was very quickly suppressed by the University authorities. Hardly had he settled in Brussels a year or two later, with a view to studying for the legal profession, than he definitely renounced the law and flung himself with all the ardour of a highly-strung temperament into the literary movement of the capital. From that day to this his pen has never been idle. The pages of *L'Art Moderne* and of contemporary periodicals bear witness both to his diligence as a critic and to the sanity and generosity of his literary appreciations.

In art, Monet and Renoir awakened his early enthusiasm ; specimens of his more mature and detailed art criticism are to be found in two small volumes dedicated respectively to the painting of Fernand Knopff and J. Heymans. But it is emphatically as a poet and not as a *prosateur* that Verhaeren has made his name. Year by year he has issued in rapid succession a series of 'plaquettes,' slim quarto volumes of verse, printed on rough-tinted paper, and now, for the most part, long out of print. I give them in the order of their publication : the very names are full of a weird suggestiveness—*Les Flamandes, Les Moines, Les Soirs, Les Débâcles, Les Flambeaux Noirs, Les Apparus dans mes Chemins, Les Campagnes Hallucinées, Les Villages Illusoires, Les Villes Tentaculaires,* and, within the last year, a drama, *Les Aubes*.[1] The soul's growth of the poet may be traced throughout the series, and his life's history is laid bare to those who would read.

As certainly as Maeterlinck is the represen-

---

[1] Recently translated into English by Mr. Arthur Symons under the title *The Dawn* (Duckworth).

tative dramatist of his country at the close of this nineteenth century, so is Verhaeren the representative lyric poet. It is impossible to avoid bringing the two names into constant juxtaposition. Both men are the product of one and the same literary movement, and both are characteristic of their age and their country. Verhaeren, though to-day only in his forty-fourth year, has been in turn materialist and symbolist, the poet of blind revolt and the poet of mystical faith, the passionate lover of beauty and the morbid delineator of life in its most hideous aspects. But throughout the ever-varying emotions of an intense and poetic temperament, capable of appreciating at one moment the purest and most ecstatic joys, and at another of wallowing in the blackest and most unrelenting misery, we can trace the strong and lasting influences of his early surroundings and his Flemish birthright. Born at St. Amand, not far from Antwerp, his boyhood was spent on the mist-laden banks of the Scheldt, in the midst of that flat, wide-spreading, dyke-bound Flemish landscape, 'la verte immensité des plaines et des plaines,' which possesses indeed a beauty and a poetry of its own, but is also pervaded by a haunting melancholy. It is a landscape to render a thoughtful boy still more thoughtful and dreamy, to develop in him a love of silence, of immensity, of austere beauty, and to encourage him to penetrate by slow degrees into the hidden secrets of nature, the great mystical lessons of life. All these characteristics have been Verhaeren's throughout his career, marking him off as Flemish by birth. Yet there are in his complex nature other characteristics—his nervous temperament, his gloomy outlook on life, his instinctive sense of colour—which would lead one to suppose, and there is nothing extravagant in the supposition, that there is a streak of Spanish blood in his veins. To his century, or rather to this latter end of our nineteenth century, belong his intense subjectivity, his lack of moral reticence, his morbid love of self-analysis, amounting at times almost to insanity. The eternal 'Moi' of the supreme egotist dominates too many of his pages, yet so pathetic are his revelations, so soul-stirring the pictures he paints in glowing language of his soul's suffering, that the sternest moralist must fain forgive him a self-concentration turned to so artistic an account. As a poet he is gifted with an almost extravagant imagination, a passion for harmonious sounds, a vivid power of snatching fleeting impressions, of reproducing rapid action, of painting a gesture; and to these he has added of recent years an exquisite sense of the mystical beauty of life, and a subtle gift of symbolical representation. His friend and critic, Albert Mockel, hails him as the 'poète du paroxysme,' a term which admirably renders the leading characteristic of one period of his life, but which only recognises a single and, in my opinion, by no means the highest aspect of his poetical faculties. But without having passed his poems in review, it is not easy to arrive at any true estimate of his genius.

Curiously enough, Verhaeren started on his literary career as a materialist. There is a Zolaesque quality about some of his early work; and in *Les Flamandes*, his first published volume of verse, there are descriptive poems of Flemish village life that read like a page of *Germinal*. He sees with that passion for detail which has never left him, and he reproduces with a faithful accuracy and with a vigour of language that commands our admiration, but he prefers to linger over the least attractive aspects of peasant life, its coarse brutality and superabundant flesh and drunken revelling. His *Flamandes* are the women that Rubens painted ; his village scenes those that we are familiar with in the canvases of Jan Steen ; but, as a rule, without atmosphere, without inspiration, and so without charm. Happily, the materialistic stage did not last long, and there are already glimpses of higher things in *Les Moines*, the outcome of a visit to a Trappist Monastery in Hainault. Verhaeren's monks are solid, square-shouldered Flemish peasants, strong and fiery, triumphing over their animal passions, or again, simple, benign, and placid, 'les amants naïfs de la Très-Sainte Vierge.' But he is mainly inspired by memories of the mighty abbots

and priors of the Middle Ages, the rivals of
kings and barons, the civilisers of nations,

'Abatteurs d'hérésie à larges coups de croix.'

The life of the modern recluse is too uniform
and cramped for his taste; he loves space and
size, and giant sins and boundless repentance,
and his sympathies are only really aroused by
something vast, mighty, infinite. So, too,
he loves the outward pomp and dignity of
ecclesiastical functions as representative of the
universality of the power of the Church. In
spite of a certain monotony of form, *Les
Moines* is full of beautiful and sonorous
rhymes and subtle observation of line and
colour. But even so the young poet does
not penetrate far below the picturesque exteriorities of cloistered life, of the cowled monks
in choir and cell. Of the hidden mystical life,
the life of prayer and renouncement so marvellously shadowed forth in *En Route*, we find
traces only here and there. Yet it is only fair
to remember that *Les Moines* belongs emphatically to the apprentice stage of the poet's career,
and as such it is full of power and promise.

A chasm, both moral and intellectual, seems to divide all Verhaeren's previous work from *Les Débâcles* and *Les Flambeaux Noirs*, published some years later. It is these powerful, gloomy, and lurid volumes which have earned for their author the epithet of 'poète du paroxysme,' and which by many of his admirers are regarded as indicating the high-water mark of his genius. I confess that I have never been able to share this view. I prefer to regard these years of despair and gloom in the life of the poet as a transitional period, years of *Sturm und Drang* through which he had to pass in order to rid himself of his early materialism before passing into the higher stage of mystical communion with nature, which is the prevailing note of *Les Villages Illusoires*. *Les Débâcles* seems to me to mark a stage, not a result, and it had for its external cause a prolonged nervous crisis, the result of ill-health. From the moral point of view the volume is utterly morbid, hysterical, and self-centred, the outcry of a suffering soul in desperate revolt against fate. For the time at least the black cloud of despair has descended upon him. In his own words, he is 'immensément emmailloté d'ennui'; 'le néant' reigns supreme. He rakes over all the emotions of his being, only to discover no cause for hope. He calls upon himself to triumph over his despair, only to fall back more deeply into the slough. His imaginings become those of a maniac—

'Quand je suis seul le soir, soudainement par fois,
Je sens pleurer sur moi l'œil blanc de la folie.'

He describes his own corpse rotting in the grave; he longs to be an idol in a Benares temple before whom fanatics prostrate themselves; or again, a monk in a 'cloître de fer,' his erotic passions crushed by inhuman penance. In *Les Flambeaux Noirs* the element of madness becomes still further intensified, and the poet grows more and more incoherent. His weird ballad of 'La Dame en Noir des Carrefours' is practically a glorification of prostitution, and is characteristic of the morbidly unhealthy side of his genius. His hallucinations find their most poetic expression in a tragic poem with the constant refrain—

'Je suis l'halluciné de la forêt des Nombres,'

full of the wild and tangled imagery of an intellect tottering on the borders of lunacy. While revelling in his sufferings and his passions and his pride, he turns from time to time with longing eyes to the externals of religion, to the æsthetic calm of cathedral aisles, to the harmony of slow chanting in dark chapels, to visions of flaring candles and mitred abbots and golden monstrances, to the peace of midnight vigils, and in some exquisite lines he has himself recourse to prayer in a moment of hope which he believes to be vain :—

> 'La nuit d'hiver élève au ciel son pur calice,
> Et je lève mon cœur aussi, mon cœur nocturne,
> Seigneur, mon cœur ! vers ton pâle infini vide,
> Et néanmoins je sais que rien n'en pourra l'urne
> Combler, et que rien n'est dont ce cœur meurt avide ;
> Et je te sais mensonge et mes lèvres te prient.
> Et mes genoux ; je sais et tes grandes mains closes
> Et tes grands yeux fermés aux désespoirs qui crient
> Et que c'est moi qui seul me rêve dans les choses ;
> Ayez pitié, Seigneur, de ma toute démence
> J'ai besoin de pleurer mon mal vers ton silence !
>
> La nuit d'hiver élève au ciel son pur calice.'

But in spite of all his extravagances and incoherencies, it would be absurd to deny that as poetry, which after all is the main point, *Les Débâcles* marks a distinct advance on its predecessors. It can show an exuberant wealth of imagery, a freedom from conventional restraints, and a widening of the horizon of life over which the imagination can roam. In form, too, Verhaeren has developed many of what have remained as his special characteristics; his bold handling of the 'vers libre' in preference to more Academic forms, his predilection for polysyllabic rhymes, his haunting rhythmical effects obtained by an artful repetition and manipulation of alliterative phrases. *Les Flamandes* and *Les Moines* contained but two aspects of human existence, to which the poet restricted himself; in *Les Débâcles* he flings himself into the primary emotions of life, taking the whole scale of human experiences within his grasp; and if the result is not always edifying or beautiful or harmonious, yet we feel grateful to the poet for being true to his own self, and true, in great measure, to life. But as the ripe product of Verhaeren's mature genius, I must once more decline to accept *Les Débâcles*.

It is a positive relief to escape from these gloomy pages into the purer and clearer atmosphere of *Les Apparus dans mes Chemins*. The volume indeed opens in the minor key with renewed visions of the melancholy landscape in which the poet's soul has hibernated so long, and renewed lamentations over the death-like bondage from which there seems no escape. A series of symbolical figures passes before his eyes, 'Celui de l'Horizon,' 'La Fatigue,' 'Le Savoir,' and finally, 'Celui du Rien,' a poem at once so grotesque, so ghastly, and so hopelessly incoherent, that it reads like the lurid visions of a delirium tremens patient. Verhaeren is frequently coarse, but in this instance he passes all bounds. Then suddenly the clouds of despondency roll asunder, and the sunshine of hope irradiates the landscape in the beautiful poem 'Saint-Georges.' So vivid is the picture of the radiant knight sweeping down from heaven in all the panoply of war to the deliverance of the suffering soul below, so joyous and triumphant is the rhythm of the short resonant lines, so tender the gratitude of the soul dragged forth from its slough of despond, that the poem must surely commemorate some spiritual crisis in the life of the poet himself, some sudden awakening to the infinite possibilities of human existence. It was a charming and felicitous fancy to symbolise his conception of hope in the warlike figure of the legendary saint who triumphs by courage and purity over the dragon of sin and despair. No English poet, to my knowledge, has paid such graceful and reverent homage to our national saint—

> 'Ouverte en tout à coup parmi les brumes
> Une Avenue!
>
> Et Saint Georges, fermentant d'ors,
> Avec des écumes de plumes
> Au chaufrein tors de son cheval sans mors
>
> Descend.
>
> . . . . .
>
> Il sait de quels lointains je viens,
> Avec quelles brumes dans le cerveau
> Avec quels signes de couteau
> En croix noire sur la pensée,
> Avec quelle dérision de biens,
> Avec quelle puissance dépensée
> Avec quelle colère et quel masque et quelle folie
> Sur de la honte et de la lie!
>
> J'ai été lâche et je me suis enfui

Du monde en un grand moi futile ;
J'ai soulevé sous des plafonds de nuit
Les marbres d'or d'une science hostile
Vers un sommet barré d'oracles noirs.

. . . . .

L'aube ouvre un beau conseil de confiance
Et qui l'écoute est le sauvé
De son marais, où nul péché ne fut jamais lavé.
Le Saint Georges, cuirassé clair
A traversé par bonds de flamme
Le doux matin parmi mon âme ;
Il était jeune et beau de foi,
Il se pencha d'autant plus bas vers moi
Qu'il me voyait plus à genoux ;
Comme un intime et pur cordial d'or
Il m'a rempli de son essor
Et tendrement d'un effroi doux ;
Devant sa vision altière
J'ai mis en sa pâle main fière
Le sang épars de toute ma douleur ;
Et lui s'en est allé m'imposant la vaillance
Et sur le front la marque en croix d'or de sa lance
Droit vers son Dieu, avec mon cœur.

The same spirit of freshly awakened hope pervades the subsequent poems of the volume. The whole landscape is changed, or rather, it is gazed upon with changed eyes. The plain is bathed in sunshine ; the north winds have fled, and the poet meets in his wanderings with tender saint-like figures, blue-robed Mercy, and white Virtue, and pensive Love, who talk to him with—

> 'De belles voix douces et consolantes
> Comme leurs robes et leurs mantes
> Long-tombantes et longuement calmantes.'

The lines are illustrative of the hypnotically soothing effect of harmoniously repeated sounds, an effect in the use of which both Verhaeren and Maeterlinck are past masters.

In another poem the poet meets with his Angel Guardian, pure and calm, the hem of her robe embroidered with the three theological virtues, seated in the midst of luxurious blossoms. He lingers lovingly in some of the most exquisite lines he has penned over the sunny garden landscape, gay with bright flowers and green sward and butterflies, symbolical of the new life that has dawned in his soul. Thus it becomes evident that Verhaeren is tentatively launching his skiff on the deep waters of mysticism. He has come to see that the relation of man's conscience to life is all-important, and that the outward and visible manifestations of nature are mainly beautiful and interesting in so far as they give evidence of their inward and spiritual meaning. For the mystic the realities of life fade into the background; the spiritualities are omnipresent. Verhaeren's mysticism, however, is neither theological nor ascetic, nor, it must be confessed, very profound—rather it is the graceful sympathetic mysticism of the dreamer, whose tender susceptibilities are being continually jarred by the material brutalities of life, and who turns for consolation to joys and appreciations of which the uninitiated can have no perception. There is no conversion—to use the hackneyed phrase—in all this; it is the natural development of the poetic temperament purged by a period of suffering. Yet *Les Apparus dans mes Chemins* undoubtedly marks a turning-point in the poet's life. Henceforth he gazes outwards rather than inwards, and his genius takes a wider flight.

The work which the poet himself, I believe, regards as his most noteworthy production, is a Trilogy consisting of two volumes of verse, *Les Campagnes Hallucinées* and *Les Villes Tentaculaires*, and his recently published drama *Les Aubes*. It is his longest and most ambitious effort, written throughout in a tragic and prophetic spirit, and undoubtedly contains much admirable and striking work. But for my own part, with all due respect for the Trilogy, I prefer Verhaeren in his lighter moods—moods which have already produced *L'Almanach* and *Les Villages Illusoires,* and still more recently, a volume entitled *Heures Claires.* Yet even at his gayest there is an unmistakable strain of melancholy running through everything that falls from the pen of the Flemish poet. A distinctive note of many of his later poems is the sense of death by which they are pervaded; of death and of madness, which lurk in the darkening landscape, and to which sooner or later man falls a helpless prey. Death is ever relentless, merciless, omnipotent; nothing can avail against her, not even 'La Sainte Vierge,' to whom the peasants turn in their despair. It is here that Verhaeren and Maeterlinck approximate most nearly to one another. To both the spirit world has become the real, the dominant world, and man in his material form, in his outward and visible being, is the mere sport of the infinite and

immeasurable forces which surround him, which
he feels dominating his life, but of whose personality
he remains necessarily in ignorance.
Freewill becomes almost blotted out from life;
we are all at the mercy of these dimly perceived
influences, and more often the evil triumphs
over the good. Yet there is Beauty in life to
save us from despair—abstract Beauty, invincible
in her strength and soul-satisfying in her
manifestations. Beauty is nature, undefiled by
man, the virgin plain which the *Ville Tentaculaire*,
or modern industrialism, is eating up.
Man's works for the most part are evil; he is
fallen humanity, with material instincts, a lust
for gold and animal passions. Yet he is
possessed of a soul, and those who will may
commune with Nature, and so rise to some
measure of appreciation of the higher mystical
life. Verhaeren points no moral in all this—
the poet is not concerned with results—he
simply paints life as it appears to him, and
would disclaim responsibility for the sadness
of his pictures. For himself, he finds his
happiness in the conviction that a benign spirit
from beyond the grave watches over and directs

his life. He feels her hand in his hand, her robes brush past him, her eyes gaze into his, and the forlorn hopelessness of his former life is transformed into an energising passion of love and gratitude.

Such, in very inadequate outline, is the poet's later attitude towards life. To this period belongs *Les Villages Illusoires*, which has always seemed to me at once the most beautiful and powerful of his works, most full of true poetical feeling. But I advance the opinion, not without diffidence, for I find that it is not shared by his admirers among *les jeunes* either of Paris or of Brussels, to whom he appeals most strongly as the poet of revolt, in blind conflict with fate. Such a mood, however, is as a rule unsympathetic to the English temperament, and I still think that when the English public rises to an appreciation of Verhaeren it is *Les Villages Illusoires* rather than *Les Débâcles* or the Trilogy that will be best appreciated on this side of the Channel. In painting these illusory villages, his symbolism finds its most perfect expression. With delicate art and with a wonderfully minute appreciation of the conditions of labour, he selects the humble toilers of the plains as symbols of the primary truths of life. Many of the poems are protests against selfish, narrow, and materialistic aims. He writes with bitter scorn of the Carpenter who settles all the problems of life by rule and line, and can realise nothing outside his own petty mathematical calculations. *Les Pêcheurs* gives a weird picture, full of suggestive teaching, of the fishermen fishing with bent backs in stagnant waters through the misty night. So absorbed are they, each in his own selfish labours, that though side by side, they never see one another, or speak to one another, or help one another. Of the enthusiasts and visionaries, the idealists of this world, even though their labours be barren and their dreams impracticable, Verhaeren writes with a note of triumphant tenderness. We find it in the beautiful and pathetic poem of the Ferryman rowing vainly against time and tide in answer to a distant voice from the clouds, and again in more dramatic form in the Bell-ringer wildly tolling his bell in the tower when the church is in flames. It is one of the poet's finest word-pictures, this of the old man, a martyr to duty, the flames 'les crins rouges de l'incendie' encircling the tower until with a crash he is buried in the ruins. Here is a finely-conceived incident of the conflagration:—

> 'Le vieux sonneur sonne si fort qu'il peut
> Comme si les flammes brûlaient son Dieu.
>
> . . . . .
>
> Les corneilles et les hiboux
> Passent avec de longs cris fous
> Cognant leurs têtes aux fenêtres fermées
> Brûlant leur vol dans la fumée
> Battus d'effroi, cassés d'essors
> Et tout à coup, parmi les houles de la foule
> S'abattant morts.'

Most profound of all in conception, and most illustrative of the mystical optimism of the poet's later mood, is *Les Cordiers*. Stepping always backwards, twisting the pale hemp in endless strands, the rope-maker seems to draw down upon himself the horizons of life, and reads the past, the present, and the future: the wild, free passionate life of the past crowned by 'la mort folle et splendide'; the present, with its materialism, its pride of intellect, its miracles of mechanical invention replacing the miracles of Faith; and the future, a double golden staircase of Hope and of Science leading upwards to where Faith unseals the eyes of all, and all are united in a universal peace.

In melodious rhythmical verse nothing, it seems to me, surpasses Verhaeren's word-pictures of the elements, giving to each its peculiar quality of mournful beauty, whether he sings of the rain—

> 'La pluie,
> La longue pluie avec ses ongles gris,'

or of ' The fierce wind of November,' or of the infinite heavy monotony of a fall of snow—

> 'La neige tombe indiscontinûment
> Comme une lente et longue et pauvre laine
> Parmi la morne et longue et pauvre plaine
> Froide d'amour, chaude de haine.'

English versions of all these studies of nature are to be found in a little volume of translations from Verhaeren from the pen of Miss Alma Strettell—translations which convey the spirit and the rhythm of the French with a rare felicity. Here is a picture of the Flemish landscape taken from the poem 'La Pluie,' from which scarcely anything of the haunting power of the original is lacking—

> 'The rivers through each rotten dyke that yields

> Where coils of drowned hay
> Float far away;
> And the wild breeze
> Buffets the alders and the walnut trees;
> Knee-deep in water great black oxen stand,
> Lifting their bellowings sinister on high
> To the distorted sky;
> As now the night creeps onward, all the land,
> Thicket and plain,
> Grows cumbered with her clinging shades immense,
> And still there is the rain,
> The long, long rain,
> Like soot, so fine and dense.'

But Verhaeren's finest poem in this strain is 'Le Silence,' showing the boundless stretch of heather-grown plain, over which hovers a silence that can be felt. Nothing has broken it since the last thunderstorm of summer. Here and there a church bell tolls, here and there a waggon creeps slowly past. I quote again from Miss Strettell's admirable translation—

> 'But not a sound is strong enough to rend
>   That space intense and dead.'

So overwhelming is the sense of silence, that those who fall beneath its spell come to regard it as a living force—

> 'Old shepherds, whom their hundred years have worn
>   To things all dislocate and out of gear,
>   And their old dogs, ragged, tired-out, and torn,

Oft watch It on the soundless lowlands near,
Or downs of gold beflecked with shadows flight,
Sit down immensely there beside the night.
Then, at the curves and corners of the mere,
The waters creep with fear;
The heather veils itself, grows wan and white;
All the leaves listen upon all the bushes
And the incendiary sunset hushes
Before Its face his cries of brandished light.'

'Le Silence' is further interesting as bringing the author into direct comparison with his friend and compatriot the late Georges Rodenbach, whose volume of verse, *Le Règne du Silence*, had a considerable success in Paris, and whose admirers frequently placed him on a level with Verhaeren, and even with Maeterlinck. In such a judgment I cannot for a moment concur. After the broad sweep of Verhaeren's poetry and the temerity of his images there is something essentially timid, restricted, even 'precious,' about Rodenbach's elegant boudoir verses, graceful and ingenious as they frequently are, and I venture to say that in the whole of his volume on Silence there is nothing half so penetrating or convincing as Verhaeren's one exquisite rhythmical poem.

The leading motive of both *Les Campagnes*

Hallucinées and *Les Villes Tentaculaires* is the destruction of the former by the latter. The constant inroads of the town on the country are as a nightmare to the poet's soul. He foresees that, stretching out its loathsome tentacles, the city will suck in and devour bit by bit the vast plain that he loves so well, and that in these later volumes he mourns over as over the body of a dead friend—

'La plaine est morne et lasse et ne se défend plus,
La plaine est morne et lasse et la ville la mange.'

In modern industrialism, with its factories and chimneys and railways and crowded docks, he can see nothing but what is hideous and revolting. He passes in review, one after the other, the features of a modern town—the theatre, the Bourse, the sailors' quarter—and he paints each in lurid colours, working himself up into a frenzy of eloquent denunciation. There is much that is incoherent in the volume, much, too, that is overstrained and laboured, as though Verhaeren himself had wearied over his subject, while here and there he becomes positively grotesque. Once or twice only he melts into a gentler mood in his descriptions, clear and vivid as an outline drawing, of the statues that adorn the town—monk and soldier, apostle and *bourgeois*, the individuality of each indicated with exquisite perception. The long poem 'La Révolte' is a veritable *tour de force*, and brings his denunciation of *la ville tentaculaire* to a climax. The misery, the vice suddenly explode, and revolution sweeps all before it. At such a moment Verhaeren has all the dramatic instincts of Victor Hugo, whom he curiously resembles. The rush of the maddened people, the lust for blood, the sack of churches, the torches with tongues of flame setting fire to the buildings, oppress the reader with an irresistible sense of reality. Anarchy lives in his powerful lines; it is a dramatic moment rendered with infinite art.

Curiously enough, the dramatic instinct which is so conspicuous a trait in many of his shorter poems seems to have forsaken the poet as soon as he turned his attention to a professedly dramatic work. At best, *Les Aubes* is a play to be read in the library; I cannot believe that it could ever pass successfully through the test of a theatrical performance. It is entirely lacking in any magnetic quality. I must confess, too, that the precise intention of the play escapes me. The situation seems to be that of the Paris Commune—the enemy outside the gates of Oppidomagne, and the populace in revolt within. The town has eaten up the country, and there is famine in the land. The tribune, Jacques Hérénien, the friend of the people, personifies the new Justice, which is to be the salvation of nations. He opens the gates of the city to the enemy, who make common cause with the people against their rulers; but in the temporary disorder that ensues Hérénien is slain. The victory demanded a victim, and it is over the grave of the leader that a new era dawns for humanity. Presumably, the poet intends to herald some Socialistic millennium, but it is not easy to discern on what he bases his hopes. The play has all the possibilities of a great dramatic situation; it has here and there fine and vigorous lines, and it is written round a central conception, which clearly appeals strongly to the author, yet it never for a moment takes hold of the reader. Perhaps, also, a want of unity in the form—for the author not only alternates between prose and verse, but between blank verse and rhymed—is partly responsible for the sense of disappointment with which, I am afraid, even Verhaeren's most enthusiastic admirers must have received his venture into the dramatic field.

Concerning the idiosyncrasies of Verhaeren's style, it would be easy to be captiously critical, and doubtless there is much in the form of his poems to which that august body the French Academy would sternly take exception. If a rhyme possesses the required sound, the Belgian poet does not trouble himself about spelling and terminations, or about the due balancing of masculine and feminine rhymes. It has often been alleged against him, possibly with some truth, that in point of fact he has no ear for the niceties of French prosody; and that if he has shown all his life a preference for 'vers libre,' it is because he is incapable of wielding the more delicate and highly finished weapon. He has a passion for sonorous and many-syllabled adjectives, more especially for those ending in 'aire' and 'oire,' such as 'diamentaire,' 'myriadaire,' 'ostentatoire,' and where the French language fails him he does not hesitate to enrich her vocabulary according to his needs. So, too, he takes liberties with his syntax, and makes effective use of such phrases as 'la souvent maison de ma tristesse' and 'le tout-à-coup Saint Georges.' But in spite of all that pedantic critics can allege against him, the fact remains that Verhaeren is a most skilful manipulator of the French tongue. He commands a ceaseless flow of sonorous and harmonious language, a rich vocabulary, and a rare gift for bold and picturesque imagery. In his hands the 'vers libre' becomes a marvellously flexible instrument for the use of his somewhat fantastic genius. He stands to-day in the plenitude of his gifts, on the threshold of a high reputation, and it may well be that his best work lies still before him. Any attempt, therefore, to assign him a permanent place in the literary ranks of the age would be vain and premature; yet there can, I think, be no doubt that in virtue both of the nobility of his language and the wide sweep of his imagination he is entitled to a very high rank among contemporary poets.

I should like to say that he is something more than a poet; that he is also a thinker. He appeals at once to the intellect and to the imagination; his poems bear the impress of personal suffering and personal knowledge; and they are full of suggestive thoughts on the eternal problems that arrest the attention of mankind. In a word, Émile Verhaeren is intensely human, both in his joys and sorrows, in his hopes and his despair, and it is this near sense of comradeship which evokes in the reader a strong personal sympathy for the man, in addition to the homage due to him as a poet.

MAURICE MAETERLINCK

THE literary world would be taken by surprise were one of our contemporary English playwrights—Mr. Pinero, let us say, or Mr. H. A. Jones—to undertake to instruct us in the philosophy of life. What have they to do with the mystery of existence? Yet nothing has seemed less surprising than that Maurice Maeterlinck should have wandered from the dramatic stage into the realms of contemplative thought. There is no abyss between the *Petits Drames pour Marionnettes* and *La Sagesse et la Destinée*. The synthesis of *Aglavaine et Sélysette* is contained in *Le Trésor des Humbles*. This simple fact seems to differentiate M. Maeterlinck's genius more clearly than any other from that of his contemporaries in the dramatic art. Maeterlinck is a dreamer and a thinker more than a writer of plays, a searcher after truth rather than a delineator of circumstance. If we are to understand him at all—his aims, his ideals, his attitude towards his art—we must look at his work as a whole, and seek in the pages of his prose essays for the clue with which to unravel the mystical riddles of *L'Intruse* and *Les Aveugles*.

On me, I confess, few books have exercised so great a fascination as *Le Trésor des Humbles*. It is emphatically not a volume to be skimmed through hastily and flung aside. Rather it is a book deserving of an exquisite binding, to be kept by one, that it may be studied leisurely and at one's ease, emptying one's mind of the bustling materialism of life. And under these conditions the reader may find himself transported to a new world full of mystical wonders, whose very existence hitherto he has only half suspected, now brought as it were within his grasp. I do not suggest that Maeterlinck is a profound and original thinker—rather he is a man of exceedingly sensitive perceptions, carefully and rightly cultivated, who from his childhood upwards has stood a step nearer to the unseen realities of life than the majority of his compeers. He is a poet gifted with a spark of the divine flame, but he is also a scholar for whom the great writers and teachers of the past hold marvellous secrets and eternal truths to be mastered only by humble study. Thus he possesses the charm of a wide and sympathetic culture in addition to the attraction of his own poetic gifts. And, above all, he possesses the incomparable gift of style—delicate, pellucid, harmonious, and yet with a strange tenacity of power, a haunting rhythm, and when requisite, an admirable cleanness of outline. Maeterlinck does not for an instant conceal—and hence the charge of undue plagiarism that has sometimes been levelled against him cannot, I think, be fairly maintained—the various sources from which he has gleaned those intellectual riches which he has assimilated with such happy results. He tells us frankly and gratefully in these prose essays how he has sat at the feet of Plato and Plotinus, of Marcus Aurelius and Carlyle; how he has absorbed the mysticism of paganism and the mysticism of Christianity; how he has lingered lovingly in the pure contemplative atmosphere of the Admirable Ruysbroeck and his contemporaries, has familiarised himself with the intellectual conceptions of Novalis, and has felt at home in the gentle domestic transcendentalism of Emerson, 'the kindly morning shepherd of pale fields green with a new-born optimism.' He is indeed an eclectic in spiritual matters, clinging to no school, and identifying himself with no prophet. On a foundation of Neo-Platonism, buttressed by Buddhist lore, he has laid a goodly layer of mediæval mysticism of the thirteenth and fourteenth centuries, and has superimposed a sympathetic acquaintance with the random philosophic speculations of the last two centuries, together with a special knowledge of the most recent spiritualistic phenomena and trend of thought. Yet there is nothing either half-digested or fragmentary in the ethical outcome of so catholic a course of study. Maeterlinck has a wonderful gift of facile assimilation; and to however many sources we may be pleased to trace his philosophy, the fact remains that he is at once intensely individual and essentially modern, a characteristic product of this fast-expiring nineteenth century.

Thus it is only by accident, as it were, that Maeterlinck is a dramatist; it is with the mystical side of life alone that he really concerns himself; and he does so because for him, as for every soul gifted with a sense of the unseen, no other side of life is worth troubling about. For him the palpable material objects of the universe are unimportant unrealities; the hidden impalpable influences that surround us constitute the real facts of our existence. All else is vanity, mere futility. That which he sees with his eyes, and hears with his ears, is for him of no account; his whole consciousness is absorbed in a tense effort to realise ever more clearly that which is unseen and unspoken. In life, as in death, we are at the mercy of forces which from all eternity have shaped our destinies. We do nothing of our own freewill even when we think ourselves most free, and never less than in all matters concerned with Love. For the most part, we remain voluntarily blind to these great truths; we prefer to ignore them; we are afraid to face them. Yet each of us is possessed of a soul—the divine sense of the spiritual in life—and if we would we might all live in far closer union than we do with these occult influences, and with open inquiring eyes might gaze far deeper into their mysterious depths. This closer union with the unseen does not fall to the share of the worldly-wise or the self-seeker, or even of the intellectually endowed. It is the reward of pure and honest and patient striving. It is the treasure of the lowly. The very first condition of attaining to it is silence; and, as a rule, there is nothing that we banish more ruthlessly from our lives. It is curious to note how this realisation of the beauty and value of silence, learned perhaps in the midst of the widespreading, melancholy Flemish landscape, has come to be a characteristic note of the Franco-Belgian school. Maeterlinck, Verhaeren, Rodenbach, each return to it again and again. Speech, Maeterlinck tells us in the first of these essays, is never the medium of communication of our real and inmost thoughts. Silence alone can transmit them from soul to soul. We talk to fill up the blanks in life; we talk when we feel ourselves far removed from the realities of existence, or when we wish to shroud our souls from the penetrating eye of our neighbour. This thought recurs frequently in Maeterlinck's dramatic writings. In the pathetic little play *Alladine et Palomides*, the reader will remember how when Astolaine, standing at a distance, declares to her father that she no longer loves Palomides, Ablamore calls her to him, reminding her that mere words have no meaning when souls cannot reach one another. 'Il y a un moment,' he says, ' où les âmes se touchent et savent tout sans que l'on ait besoin de remuer les lèvres.' Then he gazes into his daughter's eyes and reads there what she had intended to hide from him—that she still loves Palomides. So, too, in *L'Intruse* the weird impression is forced upon the spectator that it is in the prolonged silences rather than in the words uttered that the action develops itself.

Silence, according to Maeterlinck, is so truth compelling, so illuminative, that few of us have the courage to face it; yet without silence there can be no interchange of thought, no true life, no growth of the soul. He distinguishes, it is true, between active and passive silence, between a mere somnolent quiescent state similar to sleep, and that silence, pregnant with profound meaning, in which souls stand revealed. But this active silence may spring up at any moment from the passive state, and hence our instinctive dread of silence, and most especially of silence in companionship. The most illuminating silence of all, and the most irresistible, is the Silence of Death. Which of us, however petty our souls, can stand unmoved before it? Stated with all the force of resonant reiteration in which our mystic loves to indulge, such assertions read at first sight like some strange new doctrine. Yet who among us has not realised for himself that a sympathetic silence between friends is one of the truest tests of friendship, while it is a mere commonplace to assert the inadequacy of speech in those rare moments when we are brought face to face with the primary truths of life. Maeterlinck simply sees farther into the mystery than we could ever have seen for ourselves, and he describes what he sees with luminous felicity. Much of the trivial and tawdry vulgarity of modern life may well be due to our persistent neglect of the great lesson that the Sages of old both preached and practised concerning the golden value of silence?

Death, as every reader of Maeterlinck knows, is for him a never-failing subject of contemplation. In one form or another, the sense of death, of its nearness, its swift approach, penetrates everything that the dramatist has written. For him death is not the end, but the culminating point of life, the mould, as he expresses it, into which our life runs. In *L'Intruse*, *Les Sept Princesses*, *Intérieur*, and *La Mort de Tintagiles*, death dominates the stage; there is no action, properly speaking, independently of the ghostly visitor. In *La Princesse Maleine*, cast on somewhat more conventional lines—the play that Mr. Hall Caine could not bring himself to criticise seriously because it had been compared by Octave Mirbeau to *Macbeth*, a comparison so obvious that it would 'sauter aux yeux' of the veriest schoolboy—everything is subordinated to the long-drawn-out murder of the princess in what is surely one of the most haunting and powerful scenes ever penned by an author of twenty-five. And even in *Pelléas et Mélisande,* and in the later *Aglavaine et Sélysette,* both of which are cast in a lighter mood of almost tender gaiety, the wings of death hover relentlessly in the surrounding shadows. So it is in *Le Trésor des Humbles.* The haunting presence makes itself felt on every side, even though disguised under a multiplicity of symbols. In an admirable page—a sermon on pure Christianity—Maeterlinck writes of death, 'the great reconciler.' But he is perhaps most happy of all in a wonderful chapter, beautiful in its tender pathos, on 'Les Avertis,' those who are predestined to an early grave. Nowhere is his gentle, mystical suggestiveness more convincing than here, in his presentment of these young souls, the conscious victims of a precocious doom, that all foresee, but that none dare speak of, passing swiftly and silently through life, keeping apart from the healthy throng, the vision of death shining out of their clear eyes. The whole idea, it may be argued with reason, is a mere poetic fancy; but, in the words of Aglavaine to Méléandre, 'c'est avoir si peu de chose que d'avoir raison'; and few, I think, after reading Maeterlinck's limpid prose, will care to maintain that life is not the richer for the fancy, if indeed it be nothing more.

There is, however, a more cheerful side to Maeterlinck's mysticism, a gentle optimism, the outcome probably of his inherited Catholicism, and a simple faith in a regenerated humanity in which one may detect the influence of the pure other-worldliness of Ruysbroeck. The chapter on 'La Bonté Invisible,' an ardent plea for the encouragement within us of those secret instincts which make for goodness, but which the outer, material world seems to take a pleasure in crushing, is written in his happiest mood, and is inspired by an exquisite refinement of perception. He dwells emphatically on the regenerating influence that souls may mutually exercise over each other by the mere fact that at a certain moment they 'ont été bonnes ensemble'—surely a beautiful thought. And he accords a generous recognition to the spiritual supremacy of the female sex. Woman, Maeterlinck declares, is more amenable to Fate than man, and never fights sincerely against it. She dwells closer to the feet of the Inevitable, and knows better than man its familiar paths. She possesses, too, a nobler and fuller conception of love. For her, ideal love is always eternal, and the lowest of wantons remains susceptible to its purifying influence, and may be lifted to marvellous heights of self-abnegation by a spark of the divine flame. Hence it is chiefly in communion with woman that, of a sudden, there flashes across man 'a clear presentiment of a life that does not always run on parallel lines with our visible life,' and it is often a woman's kindly hand that unlocks for him the portals of mystical truth. I confess that I follow him with less sympathy in the chapter on 'La Morale Mystique,' in which he attempts a more detailed explanation of the ideal life that exists within each of us, and maintains that our spiritual existence is absolutely untouched and uncontaminated by our material acts, for which indeed our higher nature is not to be held in any way responsible. Here Maeterlinck most decidedly parts company with his favourite Ruysbroeck, and identifies himself with one of the many mystical heresies of the Middle Ages. It is the carrying to an extreme conclusion of the doctrine of Quietism. 'The soul,' he says, 'will feel no shame for that which she has not done, and she will remain pure in the midst of some terrible murder.' And again, 'A man may have committed all the crimes held to be most vile, and yet the blackest of them may not have tarnished for a single instant the atmosphere of fragrance and of immaterial purity that surrounds him.' It is perhaps as well that he confesses a little later that in this matter of 'spiritual sins,' and of our soul's ultimate responsibility, he does not feel competent to speak; that he, and we, can as yet only see 'as in a glass darkly,' and that all save those few who have scaled the mystical heights must wait for further light.

In his most recent work, *La Sagesse et la Destinée*, Maeterlinck has attempted to go a step further than in his earlier essays; to weave all his delicate perceptions of the hidden life into a logical whole. He preaches a form of spiritualised stoicism, a moral philosophy which, though abjuring dogmatic Christianity, is none the less founded on Christian ethics and sentiment. His attitude towards life has become modified in more than one respect. The tinge of an almost Eastern fatalism that lay over all the preceding volume has disappeared from the later one. Destiny is no longer the arbiter of man's fortunes; it can be won over, modified, frustrated even, by wisdom. Maeterlinck reiterates that the interior life alone is of importance; that external catastrophes are of no account save in the influence they exert on our souls. If we are crushed by them, if we learn no lessons from them, they have been of no avail. What man calls destiny is frequently only his own weakness or ignorance to which he falls a victim. There is, our author asserts, no such thing as *interior fatality*. 'Wisdom possesses the will power to rectify all that does not deal a deathblow to the body.' He points to Œdipus as a man conquered by destiny, to Marcus Aurelius as one lifted above misfortune by wisdom. It is not in the power of destiny to prevent the soul from transforming each single affliction into thoughts, feelings, and treasure which shall remain inviolate. And so the reader is brought to the consideration of the mission of suffering in life. The wise man, we are told, suffers with the rest, for suffering is one of the elements in wisdom. He suffers perhaps more than most men, for his nature is more complete. But he understands that it is not suffering that he should seek to avoid, but the discouragement and the fetters that it brings to those who receive it like a taskmaster instead of as a messenger sent foward by a higher power whom a bend in the road hides from our view. Yet, having brought the reader thus far along the Christian road, Maeterlinck stops short of any general recognition of asceticism as a regenerating force. A certain *joie de vivre* pierces through his austere moralising, and he protests against any curtailment of man's natural faculties for earthly happiness.

Begun, we are told, as a simple essay of a few pages, *La Sagesse et la Destinée* expanded by slow accretions into a well-filled volume. Its literary form has suffered not a little in the process. Taken as a whole, there is a want of clear outline in the scheme of the work. The author is discursive, disconnected, and eager to record every thought as it floats upwards to the surface of his brain without always waiting to harmonise it with previously recorded impressions. The wonderful charm of *Le Trésor des Humbles* lies partly in its detached quality; it is full of an unexpected suggestiveness; it binds the reader to no system, but it opens up endless vistas for private exploration. In the later volume, on the other hand, the reader is a little fatigued by attempting to follow through many windings a train of thought of which the connecting links have not always, I fancy, been very distinct to the author himself. Taken as a philosophy of life, the book lies open to much wide discussion; it is perhaps more fair to accept it gratefully as a yet further instalment of those tender, subtle, and suggestive thoughts on life with which the dramatist has enriched almost every page of his writing. A delightful feature of the book is to be found in the wealth of illustrations with which the author elucidates his theories, and in the clear application he gives of certain truths which in their general acceptation are almost trite, but which come home to us with an unsuspected force from the new aspect with which he invests them. Here and there Maeterlinck has seemed to me to suggest points of contact with another thinker and dreamer on life's mysteries—a thinker far more profound if endowed with more limited sympathies—and there are pages in *La Sagesse et la Destinée* which in their detached philosophy of thought remind one of those paragraphs of delicate cultured wisdom which the late Mr. Coventry Patmore collected under the title of *The Rod, the Root, and the Flower*. But where Maeterlinck is confessedly still a searcher after knowledge, a patient unraveller of the tangled web of life, Patmore writes as one holding in his hand the key that unlocks the portals of universal truth.

So far I have attempted very imperfectly to indicate Maeterlinck's general attitude towards life. There springs from it naturally his special attitude towards literature and his conception of the part that literature should play in our existence. It has been the secondary object of these essays to clear up whatever of mystery may have been felt by his readers to obscure the *raison d'être* of his own dramatic writings. For Maeterlinck the highest function of art and of literature lies in the revelation of the existence of our hidden life, in the crystallisation in concrete form of fleeting, impalpable truths, in the making visible that which we cannot see. Thus art and literature—no distinction can be drawn between them—should be more intimately concerned with the mysterious secret instincts of the soul than with the conceptions of the intellect, or even with the primary emotions of the heart. The great poets of the human race have ever been a powerful medium through which average humanity has gained such knowledge of the divine as we have hitherto acquired. By them the horizon of the human soul has been enlarged. Maeterlinck holds it as clearly established that at certain ages in the history of humanity, man's nearness to the unseen has been closer than at others—in ancient Egypt, in ancient India, in Europe during the two mystical centuries of the Middle Ages, and, he might surely have added, in the Ireland that gave us her national folklore. At such times, he tells us in his essay on the 'Awakening of the Soul,' it would seem as though 'humanity were on the point of lifting, however slightly, the crushing burden of matter. . . . Men stand nearer to themselves and nearer to one another; they see and love one another with a more solemn earnestness, a more intimate fellowship. They understand all things —children, women, animals, plants, inanimate objects—with a greater depth, a more pitiful tenderness.' Such periods have always been prolific in a glorious art, an imperishable literature. 'The statues and paintings and writings these men have left us may not be perfect, but a mysterious power and a secret charm that I cannot define are imprisoned within them, and bestow upon them a perpetual youth.' In this category he would certainly include the three authors whose writings he has translated and edited, and on whom he contributes luminous essays to this volume: Emerson, Novalis, and his own mediæval fellow-countryman, the Admirable Ruysbroeck. All three, he tells us, have penetrated far beyond the recognised circles of ordinary human consciousness, and each has discovered for himself new and strange truths—Ruysbroeck amid the blue heights of the soul, Emerson in the more accessible regions of the heart, Novalis in the domain of the intellect—truths which have made life richer for us all. On the other hand, Maeterlinck is obliged to admit that in certain centuries which have been undeniably distinguished by the pre-eminent perfection of their artistic expression, the soul has been shrouded in darkness, and intellect and beauty have been allowed to reign supreme. Such, roughly speaking, was the case in the periods marked by the great classic literatures of Greece and of Rome, and in modern times by that of France. Perfect as their literary form may have been, something, he maintains, is missing, an indefinable mystery at once tender and penetrating, which endears to our hearts works of less regular beauty. He indicates his meaning more clearly by a reference to Racine. Admitting, he says, that Racine is the infallible poet of the feminine heart, who would dare to maintain that he has ever advanced a single pace towards the feminine soul? What could we reply if we were questioned concerning the souls of Andromache or even of Britannicus? The characters in Racine's plays have no depths beyond what is conveyed by their own words. They have no 'invisible principle.' The criticism, it must be confessed, is absolutely convincing, and it has for us the further interest of clearly differentiating the French poet from our own Shakespeare. *Hamlet, Macbeth, King Lear* are all quoted in these essays as filled with 'the mysterious chant of the infinite, the threatening silence of souls and of gods, eternity thundering on the horizon, fate and fatality perceived interiorly without any one being able to say by what signs they have been recognised.' There is no sense of the mystery of life in the classical authors of France.

It is upon a fresh period of spiritual efflorescence and nearness to the unseen that, according to Maeterlinck, we are entering to-day, a period in which the dominion of the soul will expand, and it will stand revealed in all its strange strength. He believes that in the near future our souls will be able to hold communion together without the intermediate aid of the senses; and that a transcendental psychology, of which we have at present no conception, will make clear to us the relations that, unsuspected by man, have ever existed between them. Rendered thus into plain and prosaic English, the mystical expectation does not, I admit, commend itself to the average reader by any inherent probability. For Maeterlinck, however, the promise of this spiritual renaissance is to be seen on every side: not only in the general revolt against materialism and in the renewed attention bestowed upon occult laws and upon all spiritualistic phenomena, such as magnetism, telepathy, and levitation, but also in the most modern of music, in the pictures of certain artists, and in a new and nascent literature, the summits of which are illuminated by a strange glow. Elect souls have long realised that there is a tragedy in our daily life far more profound and in far closer harmony with our real selves than the tragedy that lies in great adventure. Nay, more, that the true tragedy of life—normal, profound, and universal—probably only begins at the point at which external adventures, dangers, and sufferings have ceased. For them, and emphatically for Maeterlinck himself, normal states of feeling and living are of far greater interest, and are adorned with a far more exquisite beauty than exceptional conditions and violent emotions. Hence a great artist no longer paints battle-scenes and assassinations, because the psychology of victory and of murder is elementary and exceptional, and because the futile uproar of a deed of violence stifles the timid inner voice of men and of things. Rather he will choose a peaceful landscape, an open doorway, hands lying at rest, because by means of such subjects he can add to our consciousness of life. So it is with poets, with musicians, and with all really great novelists. Dramatic art alone, in modern times, Maeterlinck affirms, has remained untouched by this sense of the hidden meaning of life, and hence the drama exists as an anachronism in this final decade of the nineteenth century.

'When I go to the theatre,' he writes in *Le Tragique Quotidien*, 'it is as though I found myself for a few hours back among my ancestors who indulged in a conception of life at once simple, arid, and brutal, of which I have scarcely any recollection, and in which I certainly have no share. I see there a betrayed husband killing his wife, a woman poisoning her lover, a son avenging his father, a father slaughtering his children, children putting their father to death, murdered kings, ravished virgins, imprisoned citizens; in a word, all the traditional fine sentiment, but, alas! how superficial and how material! . . . I came in the hope of seeing some portion of life traced back to its fountainhead and to its mysteries by connecting links that I have neither the power nor the opportunity of perceiving every day. I came in the hope of perceiving for a few moments the beauty and grandeur and solemnity of my own humble daily life, and of being shown that indefinable presence, power, or God that ever dwells with me in my chamber. I anticipated a few, at least, of those higher and better moments which I experience unconsciously in the midst of my dreariest hours; whereas, in most cases, I have merely gazed at a man who informs me at great length why he is jealous, why he has given poison, or why he intends to kill himself.'

Thus Maeterlinck, as we learn from this beautiful passage, aspires after nothing less than a complete reconstruction of the modern drama. In the near future, even on the stage, he hopes to see life in its material manifestations strictly subordinated to its spiritual subconsciousness. Plot and action are to be relegated to an entirely secondary position; the stage is to be swept clear of cheap trickery and superficial effects; and the eternal mystery of life is to rise up in an almost palpable sense before the spectator. In reply to sceptical doubts as to the practicability of his ideal, the young dramatist points to 'the august daily life of a Hamlet, who has the time to live inasmuch as he does not act,' and to the deep mystical sense underlying the words and acts of Hilda and Solness in *The Master-builder* as unique examples of that which he is striving after. And he reminds us, too, that the most celebrated of the great Greek tragedies are almost entirely devoid of action. In his own plays he has rushed, with youthful ardour, and in a noble spirit of revolt against conventionality, to a hitherto undreamt-of extreme of immobility, in order that the immaterial may unmistakably transpire; and those who have argued from this that Maeterlinck never seriously intended his dramas for representation on the stage have entirely failed to grasp his attitude towards his art. In *L'Intruse, Les Sept Princesses, Les Aveugles,* there is, theatrically speaking, no plot or action whatever; but it is this very absence of material manifestation which allows the impalpable forces of Death and Darkness and Silence to make themselves felt with such solemn and haunting effect. Even in *La Princesse Maleine,* which to a certain extent follows the recognised canons of dramatic art, and which the author would probably readily admit to have been written when his Shakespeare fever was hot upon him, the action is strangely subordinated to what perhaps I can best describe as the state of atmospheric consciousness. We feel with extraordinary intensity, piercing, as it were, the slight framework of dialogue, the pure love of Maleine and the Prince, the guilty love of Queen Anne and King Hjalmar, the conviction of all-pervading calamity advancing with swift strides, the death of Maleine, the remorseful madness of the King, the horror of sin, the irrevocable doom closing in on the haunted palace. And yet, how simple the phrasing, how elementary the construction, and how tenderly human the love passages between Maleine and her betrothed. Side by side with the indispensable dialogue there runs another, and it is this second unspoken dialogue which appeals so irresistibly to our inner consciousness.

It is because the dramatic aspirations of M. Maeterlinck seem to me so clear and unmistakable that I found myself unable to adopt as satisfactory the rendering of *Pelléas et Mélisande* given in London last summer by Mr. Forbes Robertson. Mr. Mackail's translation, it is true, was prosaic, and here and there painfully colloquial; but it was, in the main, the presentment of the play which seemed to me to rob it of well-nigh all that differentiates a play by Maeterlinck from one by every other dramatic author of our day. Produced with a scenic splendour and an elaboration of detail in accordance with the orthodox traditions of the English stage, this most charming of love idyls became little more than a drama of domestic intrigue, with here and there episodes of almost childish triviality. Its weird, elusive beauty seemed to shrivel up in contact with the material accessories of the stage. Golaud became the conventional jealous husband; little Yniold—the innocent elf-child, who brings a ray of sunshine into the gloomy castle—developed into the precocious *enfant terrible* of domestic farce; and Mélisande herself, tender, ethereal, and, above all, *inconsciente*, gave proof in Mrs. Patrick Campbell's hands of a hitherto unsuspected cousinship to the *intrigante*, to the woman with an unknown past who wrecks the happiness of a noble family. That the play was put upon the stage with the most loyal and conscientious desire to do honour to a great playwright there can be no shadow of a doubt. Yet I cannot believe that it was for no more than this that our author has worked out all his theories of dramatic art. The very essence of the play, the beautiful symbolism that underlies every phrase, seemed to have vanished into space. Pelléas alone appeared to be conscious of the hidden, unseen influences which should pierce through the enclosing envelope of the spoken word. But admirable as Mr. Harvey's acting was in the love scene of the Fourth Act, I question whether his reading was not wrong, whether the scene should not have been played throughout on a level of tender soul-communion rather than of passionate human emotion. Else there were no truth in the spiritual revelation that came later to Golaud when he exclaimed remorsefully, 'J'ai tué sans raison . . . . ils s'étaient embrassés comme des petits enfants.'

When M. Lugné Poë and the Théâtre de l'Œuvre played *L'Intruse* and *Pelléas et Mélisande* with dim lights, and lengthy silences, and slow, rhythmical movements, and—in the case of Pelléas—with a gauze veil stretched across the stage between the actors and the audience, certain of the effects may have been crude and a little incongruous, but the general impression conveyed was one of fascinating mystery and spiritual penetration. The audience may have smiled here and there at the artless simplicity of the technique and the total absence of stagecraft, but at least the beautiful cadence of the lines was preserved, the rhythmical progression of the action was felt, and the spoken word was pregnant with almost portentous meaning. And so, imperfect as the presentment may have been, I have no hesitation in believing that it was closer to the essential mind of the master than the elaborately-staged representation at the Prince of Wales' Theatre.

In *Aglavaine et Sélysette*, the latest of his works, and written subsequently to the essays, Maeterlinck seems to me to have gone a step farther than in his preceding dramas; for he has not only attempted to reproduce certain states of consciousness, but he has placed in the mouths of his characters the definite expression of his own ethical conceptions. The 'motif'—one of the elementary problems of human existence—is invested by him with a wonderfully fresh aspect. Méléandre loves his gentle child-wife Sélysette, but he also loves the wise, cultured, deep-souled Aglavaine. Aglavaine comes on a visit to the castle, reciprocating Méléandre's affection, and determined to love Sélysette as a sister. The child-wife Sélysette, who has never yet awaked to the consciousness of her own soul, because, in childish dread, she has never dared to listen to its voice, resolves to love Aglavaine for her husband's sake; and he, on his side, looks forward to a life of perfect felicity between the two ladies. So every one schemes to perpetuate this triangular idyl. But natural forces and instincts prove too powerful. Platonic friendship does not give to Méléandre and Aglavaine the happiness they crave for; and Sélysette, her soul stirred into active being by the crisis, fights down her natural jealousy, only to fall a victim to incurable sadness on realising that her own love fails to fill her husband's life. The two women rival each other in generosity; but Fate will not be baulked of his prey. Into the mouth of Aglavaine the poet has put all the mystic thoughts on life and love and the soul which he himself preaches in *Le Trésor des Humbles*; and yet, with a gentle irony, we are made to feel that it is the wise and superior Aglavaine, in the face of her noble determination that they shall all be true to their higher selves, who, in point of fact, wrecks the life of her friends. The souls of Aglavaine and Sélysette commune through silence; they read each other's thoughts in their eyes; and Sélysette grows in physical beauty as her soul expands. There are no incidents in the play—even the death of Sélysette in the last act is indicated rather than related—and the dialogue unrolled before us simply reveals the inward growth and manifestation to one another of the pure souls of the three actors. We are transported, as it were, into the region of the immaterial, into an exquisite spiritual fairyland, from which the gross materialism of the exterior world is banished. It is all very beautiful; but is it life? In the gallery of sweet, shadowy women that Maeterlinck is evolving from his poet's brain, none, I think—not even Maleine or Mélisande—quite equals in tender pathos the child Sélysette, whose baby soul is suddenly forced into maturity by the crisis in her life, and whose delicate frame succumbs to the burden over which her soul, sanctified by suffering, and strong in its new enlightenment, rejoices to the end.

Bearing in mind the nobility of the ideal that Maeterlinck has set before himself, and the fact that he has only attained to his thirty-sixth year, it seems more than probable that his great masterpiece still lies before him, and that the dramas he has already given us do not contain the ultimate expression of his genius. Their merit, in truth, does not lie in their mature perfection either of form or of thought ; rather, they appeal to me in their tender, somewhat fragmentary beauty, as exquisite tentative efforts after a conception too vast and too elusive to be imprisoned in concrete shape by the soul that has perceived it. They are like the beautiful chalk studies, suggestive of much loveliness in their very incompleteness, which a great artist will make in preparation for some mighty work of art, destined, perchance, never to see the light. In Maeterlinck's case, however, standing as he does on the threshold of maturity, there is every reason to anticipate the full fruition of his great gifts ; and even if the highest hopes of his friends were destined to disappointment, nothing, happily, could rob us of that which we already possess. From the first he has been a leader in the great revolt against materialism, which surely, whether in art or in religion, has been the distinctive feature of this final decade of the nineteenth century. He has given us a series of dreamlike idyls inspired by a tender perception of the beauty of life, and he has propounded a new theory of dramatic art in a volume of exquisite suggestiveness. To say upon the stage what has never been said before; to convey impressions which no dramatic author had attempted to reduce within the compass of eye and ear; to dispense deliberately with all those external aids and mechanical contrivances which have come to be regarded as essential attributes of dramatic representation, in order that the spiritual significance of the action may the more effectively dominate the merely external presentment,—all this Maeterlinck has essayed. I do not contend that the dramatic art of the future will necessarily be moulded on the Maeterlinck model; but honour and gratitude should be the meed of one who has proved, even tentatively, that Dumas and Sardou, Jones and Pinero have not exhausted the possibilities of modern stage-craft. If the power of symbolism is more fully recognised; if a more spiritual conception of the function of the drama is beginning to take shape in men's minds; if they are learning to grasp that as in poetry and in fiction, so also on the stage, the outward and visible semblance must be in close correspondence with some hidden invisible truth, it is largely to Maurice Maeterlinck that these things are due. For us, in England, his teaching is of no little moment, whether we apply it to contemporary drama or to the still wider field of fiction. In everything, indeed, that Maeterlinck pleads for in his essays, English literature of the present day is lamentably deficient. A vivid, instinctive perception of the spirituality of life cannot be numbered among our robust British virtues. We have neither the idealism of the Slav, nor the poetry of the Celt, nor the refined perceptions of the Latin races. We love exteriorities, we revel in photographic delineations of domestic interiors, and we have barely emerged from the backwash of the French naturalist movement. And so the influence upon us of the Flemish dramatist cannot fail to be illuminating, and the growing appreciation of his work among us is of happy augury for our literary future.

A SINGER OF BRUGES

A CHARMING writer, spellbound by the most fascinating of old-world cities, Georges Rodenbach cherished no higher ambition than that of linking his name irrevocably with that of *Bruges la Morte*. Every page that he wrote, whether in prose or verse, was a fresh testimony to a devotion that neither time nor distance could diminish. It was in the first years of his manhood that the young Belgian student forsook his native plains for the more vibrant air of Paris, where he quickly made for himself a name as a writer of refined, melodious verse, tinged with a graceful melancholy, and dignified by a sense of form. Yet in spirit he dwelt all his life in the silent, sleeping city, with belfry and béguinage, with Gothic churches and deserted streets, and green, stagnant waters. He had identified himself with its history, its art, its glorious past, its present decay. Like all the writers of the Franco-Belgian school, Rodenbach had a passion for silence, and Bruges is pre-eminently the City of Silence. To Bruges he turned for all his inspiration; his illustrations, his similes were drawn from its characteristic features; its atmosphere pervades his pages; its canals and buildings provide a background for his romances. And, very fittingly, it was to Bruges that his remains were borne for interment when, in December of last year, death brought his career to a sudden and premature close.

Rodenbach's imagination demanded no wider sphere than that supplied by the familiar features of a Flemish landscape, a Flemish interior. And amid all that was Flemish, nothing attracted him more than the beauty of the Béguinages, that most characteristic of all the institutions of his country. Every traveller in Belgium will recall those quaint Gothic enclosures on the outskirts of many of the mediæval cities where communities of women live in a semi-cloistral retirement. The long rows of little Gothic dwellings in which two or four Béguines usually reside together, facing a central grass-plot, have much of the austere charm of an Oxford quadrangle. Every Béguinage is a model of Flemish neatness and cleanliness, and a certain air of homely comfort replaces the chill bareness of the ordinary convent. Béguines are not nuns; they are free to come and go, to visit their friends, to dispose of their own handiwork. But they live together under a common rule, worship in the community chapel, and enjoy the consideration of their worldly neighbours. For the pious, solitary spinster of the Flemish middle classes the Béguinage provides at once a home and a vocation. To the simple, mediæval charm of the life Rodenbach was acutely sensitive; he loved to dwell on the quiet, monotonous existence of the Béguines, divided between prayer and innocent gaiety and the making of the beautiful lace for which the Flemish people have always shown so great an aptitude. In each of his books in turn the Béguinages play a part. It is a Béguine, Sœur Gudule, who is the heroine of the little one-act play entitled *Le Voile*, which was his sole contribution to dramatic literature, and which was acted with success at the Théâtre Français; and in his *Musée de Béguines*, a volume of short sketches, he has aimed at painting their daily life in a spirit of tender homage. Yet he has not been able to refrain here and there from insinuating into the minds of his heroines thoughts and associations more in accordance with his own mental attitude as a sceptic and a man of the world than with the solid piety of the Flemish women.

Rodenbach's poetry is descriptive and elegiac, rarely lyrical, and at times he drifted into a didactic vein. He sang, by preference, of silence and twilight, of stagnant waters and limpid eyes, of a decaying life. His attitude towards his art was entirely subjective. He himself described the colour of his mind in one of his poems when he wrote,

'Le gris des ciels du Nord dans mon âme est resté.'

Like the Flemish painters of old, he had a keen sense of the beauty of humble domestic interiors, of twilight behind muslin curtains, of the tender glow of a night-light in a sickroom, of the soothing joy of a familiar

A SINGER OF BRUGES

chamber to a troubled soul. His verses are full of the significance of the *vie des chambres*, and the simplest domestic object—a mirror, a faded bouquet—would suggest to him vague armchair reveries on life. He always wrote in a minor key, and on me, I confess, the effect is rather monotonous. Nor, in my opinion, does his undeniable grace and refinement sufficiently atone for the thinness of his sentiment, for the limited range of his muse. He made, it is true, immense strides between his first boyish productions and his two later volumes of verse, *Le Règne du Silence* and *Les Vies Encloses*, on which his reputation as a poet mainly rests; but even in these his simplicity is too artificial, his phrasing too 'precious.' He made the mistake of deliberately studying to acquire a literary manner which should express his individuality, one that should be recognisable to all his readers. In Paris, however, he has always enjoyed a higher reputation as a poet than his friend and college contemporary, Émile Verhaeren, a judgment in which I do not for a moment concur. It is founded mainly, I think, on the circumstance that Rodenbach has almost entirely eschewed 'vers libre,' which has never been a sympathetic medium to the average Gallic mind, and that he has shown himself carefully observant of the niceties of French prosody. The French nation has so profound a respect for the orthodox traditions of French poetry, that they would always give the preference to a minor poet who rigidly observed them rather than to a greater poet who occasionally set them at defiance.

A want of robustness was M. Rodenbach's main defect. His talents were all of a rather effeminate order. He lingered too long in the close atmosphere of his spotless interiors and of his low-lying, water-girt city. And the reader who accompanies him, captivated by the transparent elegance of his style, pines instinctively before long for the fresh breezes of a heather-clad hillside. As a result of his persistent study of a decaying life, however beautiful in its decay, and of his unwearied efforts to catch at the subtle significance of manifestations wholly unimportant in themselves, there is an ever-increasing tendency in his writing to unhealthy, morbid imaginings.

This is mainly true of his prose works. Often he possesses a charming fancy; at other times his sentiment is radically false, even repulsive. He creates a constant contrast, which has sometimes a piquant, but more often a jarring effect, between his own somewhat *blasé* and artificial sentiments gathered on the Paris boulevards, and his recollections of the peaceful home of his childhood. *Bruges la Morte* is full of exquisite, descriptive pages. Rodenbach has reproduced the atmosphere of the ancient city as it has never been reproduced before. But for many readers the charm of the book will be entirely vitiated by the thread of sordid, sexual passion that runs through it. The conception of the bereaved widower tracking a woman of no character through the silent streets, owing to a fancied resemblance she bore to his dead wife, deriving a sort of vicarious satisfaction from her society, and, finally, his fancy turned to loathing, strangling her with a tress of his dead wife's hair, is, from every point of view, intensely unpleasant. It is a matter of very real regret that the poet should have allowed his fancy to stray into such questionable paths.

That he could produce work of an entirely different tendency may be seen in this same volume in his delightful portrait of Barbe, the stern, old Flemish servant, who is clearly sketched from life.

As fiction, *Le Carillonneur*, one of Rodenbach's latest works, is a more ambitious effort than any of its predecessors. For the first time the author supplied a definite plot, a series of characters, and a certain unity of purpose. In both *La Vocation* and *Bruges la Morte* he had dealt with little more than a single episode. The hero of *Le Carillonneur*, Joris Borluut, architect and bellringer, is a type of the mediæval city, standing aside from the rush of modern industrial life. He lives in a world of dreams of his own creation, clinging to his native town with a passionate devotion. It is from a noble civic pride, and lest the time-honoured office of *carillonneur* should fall into unworthy hands, that he takes on himself the duty of playing the carillon on Sundays and holidays. For what would Bruges be without its carillon ringing out the old Flemish noels over the somnolent city? Borluut's real life's work lies in the restoration of the crumbling mediæval buildings of Bruges, religiously preserving their time-stained beauty. He is thus identified with the great Gothic revival to which we owe much of the beauty of Bruges to-day, and with the Flemish national movement as opposed to the French and Walloon interest, which has been one of the determining factors in the social life of Belgium during the last twenty years. Joris is loved by two sisters, daughters of Van Hulle the antiquary, another typical citizen of Bruges; by Barbe, violent and passionate, with pale face and blood-red lips, inherited from some far-off Spanish ancestor; and by Godelieve, placid and gentle, with high forehead, limpid eyes, and hair the colour of honey, like the Flemish Eves of Van Eyck and Memling. They are the outcome of the northern and the southern blood that have flowed side by side ever since Alva and his Spaniards held Flanders against the Reformers. Godelieve gives herself to Joris in the absence of Barbe, his wife; and the author, who cannot refrain from mingling religious and sexual emotions, describes her as committing this deed of treachery in a fervour of religious exaltation. It is an act inconceivable in a woman represented to us as gifted with a sweet and pure nature, and the whole episode jars on the reader's feelings. There follows the long repentance of Godelieve, culminating in the picturesque procession of penitents at Furnes, and the long expiation of Borluut, who has sacrificed his work and his love for his native town to two successive passions, neither of which brings him bliss. The story ends in gloom, black and unrelenting. The novelist was infected with the pessimism so prevalent in French intellectual circles at the present day; and although the Catholicism of his nation clung around him, and he retained to the end a sense of its symbolical beauty, it hardly subsisted in sufficiently robust form to save him from the tendencies of his generation. If Rodenbach eschewed materialism, it was because he perceived its total lack of any artistic quality, and he toyed with mysticism, realising that a sense of the unseen gave atmosphere to literary painting. At the time of his death he was still comparatively a young man, but it is probably doing him no injustice to assume that he had already arrived at the maturity of his powers. Judging him from a wider standard than that of his own immediate circle of admirers, it is impossible to deny that he was lacking in all the more virile qualities that go to make a great artist. He belonged, by the limitations of his muse, to the ranks of the 'minor' poets; and it is only fair to add that he himself would have been the first to admit the justice of the classification. He had neither Verhaeren's passionate yearning after a high ideal, nor Maeterlinck's swift insight into the spiritual significance of life. The most real thing within him was his love of Bruges; and a single passion, of so necessarily Platonic a nature, can scarcely be held sufficient to supply literary inspiration for a lifetime. Yet, as the singer of Bruges, he was so full of a tender charm, an exquisite appreciation, that his popularity in Paris as a boudoir-poet needs no explanation.

GABRIELE D'ANNUNZIO

THE love-motive in Italy predominates in life to an extent that sober northern natures cannot easily understand. Love, to the average Italian, is the aim and object of all his aspirations. Not alone the passion of a lifetime, but the most trivial caprice of the moment, is allowed to absorb his faculties, to intrude upon his business engagements, to fill his mind to the exclusion of every other consideration. No one, I think, can have lived in Italy, and have come in contact with the Italian people, without having been struck by this fundamental characteristic of Southern and Latin nature. And if it be true of men who are compelled, to some extent at least, to lead a life of mental and physical activity, it is still more true of the Italian woman, to whom, as a rule, intellectual pleasures are entirely unknown, and in whom the emotional temperament develops without restraint. In Italian fiction of the present day the love-motive is as predominant as in life. Italian novels are essentially voluptuous in tone. They treat of love in all its manifestations, and, as a rule, they treat of nothing else. Many years have passed since Manzoni wrote his tender and ever-charming historical romance; but Manzoni founded no school of fiction, and *I Promessi Sposi* will continue to occupy a unique place in the history of Italian literature. I do not think that either the religious or the historical novel has any success in the peninsula to-day, and, as far as I know, the adventure story, pure and simple, does not exist at all.

Gabriele D'Annunzio, the greatest of living Italian novelists, shares in the characteristics of his nation and his time. To me he always appears as an essential product of modern Italy, in spite of all his cosmopolitan culture. He is probably the most acute interpreter of the sex emotions of the century. His knowledge is infinite, his imagination true, his license of analysis unrivalled. Ruthless as a surgeon, with the delicate perceptions of an artist, he lays bare, through long pages of flowing rhythmical writing, the most hidden secrets of the heart, the most subtle manifestations of desire. In certain directions he has carried the psychological novel as far as it is possible for it to go. He is a consummate artist, a marvellous moulder and manipulator of the Italian language. But with all his power, with all his genius—for I think it is no exaggeration to use the word—D'Annunzio can only look on life through the medium of sex emotion. Love, passion, the attitude of man towards woman, of woman towards man, absorbs all his attention. For him life possesses no mightier secrets, no further problems. And hence, even at its very best, his work is singularly one-sided. Convincingly true within its own limits, it becomes essentially false as a representation of human life in its widest aspects. A single novel of D'Annunzio fills the reader with amazed rapture. A course of D'Annunzio produces an inevitable reaction, and I can understand its awakening in many readers a sense of nausea.

To appreciate his attitude towards his art we must bear in mind that the most fundamental trait in D'Annunzio's character is his paganism. It is an essentially Italian attribute. All through the history of Italian literature we may trace a pagan strain, an intimate connection with the classic literature of the past. It lay at the root of the whole great movement of the Renaissance. Eighteen centuries of Christianity have only crusted it over, and have never wholly eliminated it, and in D'Annunzio this old pagan spirit has burst out afresh. He is not only an Italian, but a Roman, a passionate worshipper of the city of the Cæsars, and Rome in certain aspects is still the most pagan city in Europe. D'Annunzio is wholly unaffected by the tender perfume of Christian sentiment, else had he never penned his startling paraphrases of the gospel parables. He possesses almost as a birthright that easy familiarity with the classic literature of his Latin forefathers, which to men of an alien race nothing but the highest scholarship can give. He has steeped himself in the art, the literature, the sentiment of the sixteenth century. For him beauty is the highest good, and happiness the highest goal. Christian ethics, in all matters concerned with love, simply do not exist for him. He is less immoral than devoid of all sense of morality. He is a passionate lover of the beautiful, a marvellous *virtuoso*, a singularly sensitive observer of nature. His books are full of the most exquisite descriptive pages; they are aglow with the warm Italian atmosphere. But he does not love nature for her own sake, as Wordsworth loved her. To him the budding spring, the cries of the swallow in its swift whirling flight, the silence of the mid-day heat, all whisper of human passions and human joys. Take, in the latest of his novels, the *Vergini delle Rocce*, the episode of the almond-blossom, a silvery cloud on the bare hillside, the first gift of spring, with which the hero piles his carriage as an offering to the three sisters whose hearts he deliberately plans to capture. The scene is permeated with the ineffable charm of a soft February day in Southern Italy, nevertheless the reader feels that the essential beauty of the almond-blossom lies in its symbolism of the new life that—thanks to the arrival of Cantelmo—is about to dawn for the three half-cloistered ladies of Trigento. Or turn in *L'Innocente* to the description of the nightingale's song at Villalilla, to which Tullio and Giuliana listen hand in hand at the close of their long day of reconciliation and resuscitated love.

'From the first notes it resembled an outburst of jubilant melody, a cascade of trills which fell upon the air with a sound as of pearls rebounding from the glass of a harmonica. Then there came a pause. A brilliant warbling arose, prolonged to a marvellous length, as if in a trial of strength, in a mood of defiance, as a challenge to an unknown rival. A second pause. A theme of three notes, like an interrogative phrase, passed through a chain of dainty variations, repeating the timid request five or six times, modulated as though on a slender flute of reed, on a pastoral pipe. A third pause. The song became an elegy; it changed to a minor key, grew soft as a sigh, faint as a sob, full of the sadness of a solitary lover, a heartfelt longing, a vain expectation; it burst forth into a final appeal, startling, shrill as a cry of agony; then it died away. Another and a more solemn pause. Then a new note was heard, which sounded as though it could not issue from the same throat, it was so humble, timid, mournful; it resembled so closely the chirping of newly hatched birds, the twitter of baby sparrows; then with a marvellous volubility this ingenuous accent changed into a progression of notes, ever faster and faster, which sparkled in a flight of trills, vibrated in clearest warbling, soared aloft in audacious passages, now fainter, now louder, rising to soprano heights. The songster was intoxicated by his own song. With pauses almost imperceptible, in which the notes had barely time to die away, he poured out his delirium in an ever-varying melody, passionate and tender, soft and clear, playful and grave, and interrupted now by faint sobs, by piteous lamentations, and again by sudden lyrical outbursts, by a supreme invocation.'

It appeals so passionately to the author, and he describes it so penetratingly, not merely for the beauty of the melody in itself, but because he could read into the song the intricate emotions by which Tullio and his wife had been swayed during the day. The nightingale had said all that words failed to express. I seem to feel that without lovers listening, the song of the bird would not have been transferred to the page.

Music, the most personal and the most emotional of all the arts, possesses for D'Annunzio a haunting power. It plays a part in each of his novels in turn. It is by music that lovers converse ; it is through music that the depth of their passion is revealed to the reader. Maria Ferrès plays Bach and Scarlatti to Andrea Sperelli in the days when, even to herself, she does not admit the dawning passion of her love ; and Ippolita and Giorgio Aurispa spend long hours over the score of 'Tristan and Isolde,' and afford the novelist an excuse for a dozen brilliant pages of analysis of the most marvellous drama of sex emotion ever interpreted by music. But there is a yet more intimate connection in D'Annunzio's case between the art of writing and the art of music. It is from music that he obtains one of his most characteristic effects of style. As in music a motive will recur at seemingly inevitable intervals, so D'Annunzio will deliberately repeat a phrase, sometimes with variations, but more often in the identical words, in order to bring the reader back to a previous impression, to a recurrent train of thought. The little pen-portrait of the dead uncle in the *Trionfo della Morte* is repeated at least three times in exactly the same words. The intention is to bring before the reader the features of Demetrio as they appeared to Giorgio, and it is always under one and the same aspect that a familiar face reappears to us. In the *Vergini delle Rocce* we have a line of landscape painting—the colour of the arid soil is compared to the mane of a lion—which is woven into the narrative again and again. How far this trespassing on the domain of a sister art is legitimate is a fair subject for discussion. The device is one which, in inexperienced hands, might rapidly degenerate into an intolerable affectation ; but D'Annunzio has so unerring a pen, so delicate a perception of values, that in his hands it appeals to us as singularly happy.

D'Annunzio, like Maeterlinck, is one of the precocious geniuses of the age. He is only, I believe, in his thirty-fifth year, and has therefore barely passed that 'earlier climacteric' in a man's career, from which he may measure the hopes of the future by the triumphs of the past. Yet, instead of pressing forward to new and greater victories, I am tempted to predict that the Italian novelist has already given of his best to the world. Before he was twenty he had published two slim volumes of passionate melodious verse, the *Canto Nuovo* and the *Intermezzo di Rime*, which placed him at a bound far above all his contemporaries, the veteran Carducci alone perhaps excepted. These were followed almost immediately by a small collection of short stories, *Il Libro delle Vergini*, and by further poems ; and then, at longer intervals, by his novels—*Il Piacere* in 1889, *L'Innocente* and *Giovanni Episcopo* in 1892, the *Trionfo della Morte* in 1894, and two years later the *Vergini delle Rocce*. In *La Città Morta*, which not even the acting of Sarah Bernhardt could galvanise into life when it was performed at the 'Renaissance' theatre a twelvemonth ago, we have at once his latest completed work, and his first effort at dramatic writing. The *Vergini delle Rocce* is not complete in itself; it forms but the first part of a romantic trilogy, *I Romanzi del Giglio*, the later volumes of which have still to appear. The three novels, *Il Piacere*, *L'Innocente*, and the *Trionfo della Morte*, also constitute a series of three, and have been classified by their author as '*I Romanzi delle Rose.*' They are entirely unconnected as regards incident or characters, yet they are bound together by a certain unity of purpose and conception. They represent the very best fruit of D'Annunzio's genius; of them we can judge as of a completed whole; and it is on them, I believe, that D'Annunzio's fame as a novelist will ultimately rest.

D'Annunzio has stood for the hero of each of these three novels. And as the other male characters in his books are very few in number, and are entirely subordinate to the central figure, it is no exaggeration to say that the novelist has never intimately studied or reproduced any member of his own sex save himself. This single type, then, which figures under slightly varying aspects as Andrea Sperelli in *Il Piacere*, Tullio Hermil in *L'Innocente*,

Georgio Aurispa in the *Trionfo*, and, I may add, as Claudio Cantelmo in the *Vergini delle Rocce*, represents a young Italian, sensual rather than passionate, abnormally sensitive, intensely egotistic, absorbed in his own intricate emotions, and with a mania for self-analysis. He is 'idealistic, analytical, and sophistical.' He is entirely wanting in all spontaneousness, rectitude, and simplicity of nature. He is invariably the descendant of a great race fallen on evil days, the degenerate bearer of a once glorious name. Sometimes, as in the *Trionfo della Morte*, he is physically weak; even his qualities are, as a rule, those of an effete race, and at times he hovers on the borders of lunacy, suicide, and crime.

'I was, in a word,' says Tullio Hermil of himself, 'a violent and impassioned *consciente*, in whom the hypertrophy of certain cerebral centres rendered impossible the necessary co-ordination of the spirit with normal life. A most acute watcher over myself, I yet possessed all the impulses of primitive, undisciplined nature. More than once I had been tempted by sudden criminal suggestions. More than once I had surprised myself in the spontaneous uprising of some cruel instinct.'

Yet, he is represented as retaining a certain dignity of soul through his worship of the beautiful: 'the conception of beauty is the axis of his inner being, round which all the passions gravitate,' and the delicacy of his intellectual perceptions and the refinement of his taste remain undimmed by his moral depravity.

The type is first presented to us in *Il Piacere* under the title of Count Andrea Sperelli. Sperelli is a Roman poet of noble birth in the first years of manhood. He is a disciple of Beauty, a believer in Art for Art's sake, a passionate devotee of the fourteenth century. He also worships his native Rome—the Rome of the Renaissance, of the Villa Medici, the steps of the Trinità, the Pincian Hill—and the mysterious fascination of Rome is subtly indicated. With much power of minute observation, with a few pages of exquisite descriptive writing, when the scene is transferred to the villa at Schifanoja, *Il Piacere* is, on the whole, I think, a wearisome book. It is essentially the work of a clever but immature writer, eager to display his knowledge of the world; it is crude, cynical, and pretentious, overweighted with classical allusions and artistic disquisitions, and with an irritating assumption of cosmopolitan omniscience imitated from a certain school of French novelists. Sperelli merely repels by his morbid cravings, his cynical egotism, his entire absorption in self. In its relation of external incidents the story is almost commonplace—for the life of a young man of fashion varies but little in Paris, Rome, or London—but on its psychological side it compels our admiration by the daring analysis of the emotions of the hero, of the mental sufferings he lays up for himself, of the irreparable void in a life dedicated solely to pleasure. There is but one character in the book with a touch of real nobility, the gentle, melancholy Maria Ferrès, who struggles with her dawning love for Sperelli through long pages of a delightful journal—a masterpiece of feminine idealism and weakness. But for the rest, it is simply a revelation of pitiful human depravity which no art can idealise.

In the two years that elapsed between the publication of *Il Piacere* and *L'Innocente*

D'Annunzio seems to have sprung into the plenitude of his great gifts. In the former novel there is promise, in the latter fulfilment. For me, *L'Innocente* is the one really great book that D'Annunzio has written. Both in conception and in construction it seems to me unquestionably superior even to the *Trionfo della Morte*. It was written—D'Annunzio himself makes no secret of it—under the influence of Tolstoi. A new conception of human suffering, a new realisation of the dignity of the human soul, seem to have come to him through the pages of *War and Peace*. His outlook on life has widened and deepened; he has rid himself in part at least of the clogging limitations of a materialist creed. The interest of the book is purely psychological. It tells of one of those silent tragedies in life, all the more intense and overwhelming because they are unrelieved by any outward manifestation. It is a prolonged study of two souls in their relation to one another—their sins and sufferings, their brief pathetic joys, and their long, weary expiation. There is perfect unity of interest throughout. There are no minor threads to withdraw the reader's attention from the main tragedy ; we are told nothing of how these people live, of their position, their wealth, their friends. But we follow instead the evolution of their attitude towards one another, of Giuliana's attitude towards Tullio, of Tullio's feelings towards his wife Giuliana. We are told—indeed, it is Tullio himself who relates the story, and the first person renders it all the more convincing—of his conjugal infidelities, of his debasing passion for Teresa Raffo, which dragged him away even from the sickbed of his wife, but Teresa herself never appears. We are told of Giuliana's sudden emotional frailty in relation to Filippo Arborio, but Filippo himself flits as a mere shadow through the pages, and we are never shown the lovers together. It is the effect of such actions on the inmost soul, not the actions themselves, that D'Annunzio paints. And the painting is so intensely true that the book, with all its crudeness of expression and occasional coarseness of thought, becomes convincingly moral. Inevitably, without the advent of any external circumstance, any dragged-in calamity, husband

and wife reap what they have sown. Tullio begins with a long course of studied neglect towards his beautiful wife, whom, with a refinement of marital cruelty, he treats with exquisite courtesy as a friend, a confidante, a sister, as one who could understand and appreciate his moral weakness. In the intensity of his perversion he soothes his conscience with the reflection that moral greatness being the outcome of violent grief nobly borne, his wife could never have attained to the heroic virtue which is her crowning glory save through the sufferings that he himself has imposed upon her. And for years Giuliana bears her solitude with heroic abnegation, silently, bravely, even tenderly. But at length, stung apparently into anger by continued neglect—and here, I confess, the psychology does not appear to me quite convincing—she finds a brief consolation in the love of Filippo Arborio. Tullio, at the moment when a sudden return of affection has brought him to his wife's feet, discovers that Giuliana is to become the mother of a child of which he is not the father. Nothing D'Annunzio has ever written is more impressive than the attitude of the two guilty souls towards each other with this appalling calamity overhanging them. Love for his wife, family pride, respect for his aged mother, a sense of his own original guilt, and, it must be added, a merely sensual craving for the beautiful woman he had so long neglected, all combine to keep the man silent, and the long martyrdom of the waiting months is drawn out in sickening and convincing detail. And the final murder of *l'innocente*, the hapless bastard child, that threatens by its mere presence to render conjugal life a daily torture, is effected so artistically—we forgive him the borrowing of the idea from Guy de Maupassant—that once again it is not the outward aspect of the unsuspected crime, but its inner significance, that arrests the reader.

The gloom of this tragic story is rendered all the more intense by the contrast with the background of warm Italian sunshine and peaceful rural existence which fills in the picture. It is pathetically true to life that Tullio's aged mother and his brother Federigo, whose first care is for the happiness of the young couple, should remain absolutely blind to the tragedy that is being enacted before their very eyes. Federigo is D'Annunzio's sole attempt to paint a man of high moral character and lovable disposition; and Federigo, with his appreciation of simple pleasures and his placid faith in a 'new' religion, is inspired by Tolstoi. So, too, is the fine old peasant Giovanni di Scordio, whose Slav characteristics have a curiously unreal effect in the Italian setting. The digression affords the author an opportunity for much harmonious writing on the solemn beauties of nature, but his grasp on either character is lacking in firmness. One feels that he is tentatively groping after an ideal whose beauty indeed attracts him, but which eludes his full comprehension. And a comparison with Tolstoi being thus forced upon us, it is interesting to note how differently, had he written such a story as *L'Innocente*, he would have conceived the dénouement. Without question, he would have effected the ultimate reunion and the mutual forgiveness of husband and wife through the instrumentality of the child. In its presence the past would have been blotted out in a noble, all-embracing pardon. For the Slav, with his mystical fatalism, such heights of self-abnegation do not offer insuperable obstacles ; for the sensual, clear-sighted Latin, with his acute but petty feelings, they are unattainable.

D'Annunzio spent five years working at the *Trionfo della Morte*. By universal consent in France and Italy it has been acclaimed as the greatest of his achievements. It was the *Trionfo* which first gained for its author the enthusiastic patronage of M. de Voguë, most orthodox of critics, and it was the *Trionfo* which was the first of D'Annunzio's novels to appear in an English version. Certainly it is the largest of his works both in point of size and of conception, and for this very reason it displays his weaknesses and his limitations as well as his strength. He has fallen into the prevailing fashion of making of a novel a peg on which to hang his views on every subject, a counter on which to display all his intellectual wares, however incongruous. The cosmopolitanism of his culture shows itself as a serious blot on the artistic unity of his treatment. We have Tolstoi on one page, Maeterlinck on another, and, alas, Zola on a third. Yet these are but the accidental accessories of the story, the ornaments with which he has overloaded his scheme. In its central idea it is purely D'Annunzian, and, like all its predecessors, it consists simply in the history of a man and a woman in relation to one another. The opening conversation between Georgio Aurispa and Ippolita gives the note of the whole book—the subtle struggle between hatred and desire in a purely sensual love. It is a theme in which the author's insight into the intricacies of human passion has full play. In the *Trionfo* the hero has advanced a stage further in his career of self-indulgence than in either of the preceding volumes. He is cynical, sarcastic, suspicious, bound hand and foot by his physical cravings, and yet rebelling fiercely against the chains he has forged for himself. His demands are insatiable; he exacts of Ippolita the entire surrender of mind and of soul.

'How much of you do I possess?' he asks.
'Everything.'
'Nothing, or almost nothing. I do not

possess that which I crave for. You are a stranger to me. Like every other human creature, you conceal within yourself a world that to me is impenetrable, and the most ardent passion can never reveal it to me. Of your sensations, of your sentiments, of your thoughts I know only the smallest part. Speech is an imperfect sign. The soul is intransmittable. You cannot give me your soul.'

The conviction of his helplessness drives him into brutality, into cruelty at least of speech. And slowly but inevitably the 'sudden criminal suggestions' by which Tullio Hermil felt himself to be from time to time invaded, crystallise in Giorgio into a definite homicidal mania. His uncle Demetrio, from whom he has inherited his fortune and his musical tastes, the uncle who was the sole joy of his youth, committed suicide, and in his spiritual identification of himself with his uncle suicide becomes his inevitable goal. He realises that he is ill, morally ill, verging at times upon insanity, and he has a blind hope that a true and strong love, *un amore sano e forte*, may restore his moral balance. So he and Ippolita take up their abode in a hermitage on the shores of the Adriatic, where his security of possession will be absolute and uncontested. This *Vita Nuova*, this new life, is in its outward aspects a delightful love idyl passed amid orange and olive groves by the soothing, ever-changing sea, with harvesting and grape gathering, with girls singing amid the golden furze, peasant women spinning by their cottage doors, and long processions winding through the valley to the neighbouring shrine. Yet from the first it fails to accomplish for Giorgio what he had hoped for. After the first two weeks he notes: 'Nothing in me is changed. Always the same anxiety, the same unrest, the same discontent. We are hardly at the beginning, and yet I already foresee the end.' In his craving for new sensations he is filled with ascetic aspirations, and believes himself possessed of all the necessary qualities for a life of renunciation save only the indispensable gift of faith. It irritates him to see how Ippolita's physical nature expands under the influence of the bracing air, the indolent life. Having deliberately cut her off from all outside inter-

GABRIELE D'ANNUNZIO

ests, he is revolted because her tastes and desires grow daily more puerile. He is morbidly jealous of her exuberant vitality, her frank *joie de vivre*. They have never been united by the bonds of real affection. Relentlessly his love turns to physical repulsion; the thought of the future fills him with black despair. Meanwhile Ippolita realises the change that has come over her lover, and blindly she puts forth all her feminine fascinations to bind him ever more closely to her. Feeling her participation in his inner life growing fainter, she devotes all her energies to asserting her sensual dominion. Thus she seals her doom, and the book closes in murder and suicide.

It is impossible to refer in detail to the many incidents and interpolations, quite irrelevant for the most part to the main action of the story, that D'Annunzio has been tempted to include in the *Trionfo*. It is curious that in one of his latest and most mature books a strain of naturalism should have appeared. For his whole literary attitude has been a constant protest against the supremacy of mere exteriority. Yet in the *Trionfo della Morte* there is at times a gratuitous revelling in sordid details which leaves an exceedingly unpleasant impression. Take, for example, the piteous portrait of the little, old Aunt Gioconda, steeped in piety and addicted to greediness. There is not a touch of human pity in the description, not the smallest endeavour to show the pathetic human soul behind the repulsive exterior. The notorious chapter on the pilgrimage to Casalbordino is a mere *tour de force* in horrors piled one on the other. Nothing in Zola's *Lourdes* approaches it in coarseness and in revolting detail; it is without a single redeeming feature. There has always existed a very wide license of speech in Italian literature, the outcome, I imagine, of its pagan strain, and of such license D'Annunzio, in the *Trionfo*, has taken a more unsparing advantage than in any of his previous works. Happily, there is another tendency in this many-sided book, a tendency for the first time towards symbolism, towards a mystical interpretation of life. Within the scope of his literary studies D'Annunzio has clearly included the Franco-Belgian school. In his descriptions of the peasant life around San Vito he is penetrated by a sense of the dignity of humble toil, of the sanctity of primitive sorrows, of the deep spiritual significance that lies behind child-like beliefs and old-time superstitions. The weird episode of the dying baby sucked by vampires, and that no exorcisms can release, recalls in its haunting sense of approaching death a scene from *L'Intruse*. And there is the scene of the drowned boy and his mother's outburst of lyrical grief, which is extraordinarily dramatic in its intensity of feeling.

As an interlude in the writing of romances, of which a whole new series is already advertised for publication in the near future, D'Annunzio has produced a play. The amiable ambition to attain to dramatic success is one that he shares with almost every poet and novelist of the present day. Unfortunately, the *Città Morta* has proved as little dramatic as the stage-works of poets and novelists are apt to be. All his force, all his intuitive capacity for seizing an instantaneous effect, seem to have forsaken our author as soon as he found himself at work in an unaccustomed medium. He has set himself as an ideal to be purely Greek in conception and in feeling.

He has transported a quartette of modern Italians to the thirsty plains of Argolis, with a background of Mycenæan tombs and fragmentary temples. He has conceived an incestuous passion, and has provided a blind heroine, who combines the parts of prophetess and of chorus. With such material he has essayed to build up a tragedy. Unhappily, an almost grotesque feeling of unreality pervades the whole play. The characters are little more than lay-figures performing automatic movements. There is really nothing save their names by which to distinguish Alessandro from Leonardo, both of whom entertain a hopeless passion for Bianca Maria, the sister of Leonardo. And of Bianca Maria herself I have tried in vain to arrive at any sort of realisation. The whole treatment of the situation is entirely undramatic in the modern sense of the word. Possibly D'Annunzio would tell us that such was his intention. But there should at least be a grandeur of conception, a nobility of outline, and a harmonious rhythm of movement to compensate for the lack. Here and there glowing descriptive passages have been placed in the mouths of the actors, and an almost physical sense of noonday heat has been brought home to the reader. Here and there the self-effacing, spiritually-enlightened Anna, the blind wife of Alessandro, calls to mind one of Maeterlinck's shadowy, ethereal heroines. But there is scarcely a scene which carries with it a sense of conviction. All through the drama the reader is conscious of the artificiality of the presentment, of the undisguised imitation of this writer and of that; in a word, of the unrealised ambition to re-create the atmosphere of the great Greek tragedies.

Not a little of D'Annunzio's failure as a dramatist may be attributed to his attitude towards women, and to the rôle he has assigned to them in his social presentment. Let me say at once that he has not created a single feminine character of intrinsic interest, not one that stirs our deeper feelings. His failure in this respect —surely one of the most serious that can be brought home to a novelist—is no mere accident. It has its origin deep down in the recesses of his nature. D'Annunzio accepts to the full the conventional view of the female sex that is still prevalent among the Latin nations. Woman exists for man, for his pleasures, his domestic comfort, often for his ruin; but she has no independent life, no separate entity, no ideals apart from those of sexual love. No higher possibilities for the sex have entered the mind of the novelist; even religion, save as a conventional accessory, is denied to her. Women must be gentle, tender, submissive, anticipating in all things the wishes of their lord. Giuliana's one fault was her act of rebellion against the rôle which Tullio, without the slightest justification, had imposed upon her; and unconsciously it is upon Giuliana, and not upon Tullio, that the responsibility of the catastrophe is made to lie. Morally, the women are in most cases far superior to the men, or at least to the one type of man that the author gives us. Yet they are expected to sacrifice themselves unhesitatingly to the hysteric passions of the hero. The truth is, D'Annunzio is so absorbed in self-analysis, so occupied with events in their intimate relation to his own soul, his own wellbeing, that he has not a moment in which to study humanity from an objective point of view. In a word, he never really paints character at all. As we have seen, there is not a single clearly defined, well-thought-out portrait in his whole series of novels, not one that will live in our memory. The hero is always himself; the heroine is only shown to us in her relation toward the hero. The secondary figures are but vague shadows, or are indicated merely as the individual units in a certain general impression which the author wishes to produce. Thus the whole Montaga family is created in order to convey a sense of hovering insanity; the peasantry around San Vito illustrate the effects of a mystical superstition; but in neither case does any character possess a definite individuality apart from the central conception. Somehow we seem to miss characterisation less in D'Annunzio than we should in any other author, but the fact remains that it is not there. He is entirely destitute of wide human sympathies; he seems to regard even his own creations with a cynical indifference which alienates from his own person the sympathies of the reader. He has not a word of pity for the fate of Maria Ferrès, who ruins herself for Sperelli ; or for Ippolita, who is in every sense the victim of Aurispa ; or for the three shadowy sisters of Trigento, waiting in their stately, melancholy palace for the advent of some fairy prince, women who remind me of nothing so forcibly as of delicate peaches on a garden wall waiting till the passer-by shall pluck and devour. This incapacity to regard life from the standpoint of each of his characters in turn constitutes one of D'Annunzio's gravest limitations. It seems to me to be of itself sufficient to deprive him of the right to be classed among the great constructive novelists of our time. We have been told that D'Annunzio is the centre of a new renaissance, the herald of a new dawn, the founder of a new school in the history of Italian literature. I cannot for a moment think that he is all this. Rather he is the most brilliant flower of decadence, a beautiful poisonous growth ; the product, like his own heroes, of a great nation fallen upon evil days. His writing destroys, it does not build up. It could not inspire a great cause or stimulate to high spiritual ideals. Yet, putting aside all ethical considerations, D'Annunzio has perpetrated a great and lasting literary work for his country. He has given the seal of permanency to the work initiated by Carducci, who was the first in our own day to rescue Italian lyrical poetry from the trivialities into which it had fallen by uniting a vigorous passionate spirit to the majestic forms of classic literature. To D'Annunzio is due the evolution of an Italian style. He has moulded his native language into a more perfect and more flexible instrument than when it first came into his hands. He has drawn from it unsuspected richness of form and colour. It has been the object of his daily study, of his ceaseless endeavour. And the result is a delight in rhythmical cadence, in flowing harmonies, in suavity of diction. He has gone for his models to classical sources, and he seems to me to have added much of the terse dignity of Latin to the florid grace of modern Italian. In *L'Innocente*, and again in the *Vergini delle Rocce*, his writing is at its very best; in the *Trionfo della Morte* there are here and there traces of over-elaboration, of a too determined effort to excel. He is happiest in his less ambitious moments, in his descriptions of nature, luminous as the Italian atmosphere. Sometimes with absolute simplicity of treatment he stamps an ineffaceable impression on the brain. Take the few lines on Orvieto in the *Trionfo* :—

'On the summit of a marlstone rock, above a melancholy valley, a city so silent as to appear uninhabited :—windows closed, grey alleys, in which the grass grows ; a Capuchin friar crossing a piazza ; a bishop descending from a closed carriage in front of a hospital with a decrepit man-servant at the door ; a tower against a white, rainy sky ; a clock slowly striking the hours ; suddenly, at the end of a street, a miracle—the Cathedral.'

There is in his writing a subtle quality to which no extract, and, above all, no translation, can do justice, an exquisite fluidity which carries the reader forward in a rhythmical progression. And it is for D'Annunzio's sense of style that we forgive him his sins of omission.

ANTONIO FOGAZZARO

CRITICS have questioned whether fiction is not a medium uncongenial to the Italian temperament, a mould into which the talent of the country will never freely flow. In poetry, in drama, in opera, the æsthetic aspirations of Italy have always found the fullest expression. In imaginative gifts she has never been lacking; but, until quite recently, they had not been devoted to the weaving of prose romance, or to the delineation of domestic morals. Throughout the middle of the century, when in France and England, in Germany and Russia, the production of fiction was taking on itself such wide proportions as to threaten to submerge all other branches of literary achievement, Italy remained practically silent. Earlier in the century, Manzoni had written the first, and in many respects, still the greatest of modern Italian novels, and had stepped forthwith into the front rank of European men of letters. But Manzoni was by profession a poet and a dramatist, and it was almost by accident that he wrote the novel which has made his name famous; it is noteworthy that he never wrote a second. It is only in our own day, only within the last twenty years, that a body of Italian novelists has risen up; and numerous and talented as its members are, they have founded no distinctive school of Italian fiction. Such a thing does not exist, has never existed. We find in Italian fiction traces of all the influences — romantic, idealistic, naturalist, realist, psychological—which have moulded the fiction of France during the last half century. Many examples might be summarily described as French novels written in Italian. It is as though Italian writers, filled with a sympathetic admiration for the achievements of their transalpine neighbours, had deliberately set themselves to imitate and equal that which, left to their own resources, they had never been able to initiate. Even in the delineation of his native Sicily, Verga has followed many of the methods of the realists. Matilde Serao and

F. de Roberto, while penetrated through and through with the voluptuousness which seems to form a component part of the very air of Italy, have based their novels mainly on situations with which French fiction has made us wearisomely familiar. There is singularly little character-drawing in Italian fiction, if we except the delineation of men and women under the influence of sexual passion in their relation one to the other. There is nothing of the mystery, nothing of the near sense of the spiritual in life, which make the fascination of Slav literature. In a word, Italian fiction has a very narrow scope ; in substance it has little originality ; and it does not, in any convincing fashion, portray the essential characteristics of the nation.

Happily, above the rank and file of Italian novelists there have appeared two or three who have effected all that brilliant talents can effect to supplement the lack of a national ideal in the sphere of romance. At the present time, two men are conspicuous as representing, in the essential features of their work, two permanent tendencies in Italian literature—tendencies which are necessarily antagonistic, but which have existed side by side from the days of Dante and Boccaccio. Both men are poets; and although from the circumstances of the modern literary market it is as novelists that they have attained to European fame, their talents as writers of fiction are none the less subordinate to their gifts as writers of verse. Of the place occupied by D'Annunzio I have spoken already. He is the representative of the pagan element in the Italian character; his forerunners are Boccaccio and Benvenuto Cellini and Titian; his immediate predecessor is Carducci. Fogazzaro is an idealist and a Christian; he represents the revolt against a materialistic conception of life. He has affinities with Petrarch and with the Umbrian school, and in more recent times with Manzoni and Silvio Pellico. Everywhere he paints the triumph of faith, and patriotism, and ideal love over the desires of the senses. Everywhere, on the contrary, D'Annunzio paints the triumph of passion over duty. To the author of *L'Innocente*, human passion—the desire of the man for the woman—is the most invincible thing in life; to the author of *Daniele Cortis* it is one of the feeblest. If D'Annunzio seems to us more intimately representative of what we have come to regard as a characteristically Italian conception of life, it is mainly because, in Italy as in France, the ideals of a certain section of society have received undue recognition from the prominence conferred upon them by novelists. To judge of all Italian society from the novels of D'Annunzio or Matilde Serao were almost as misleading as to judge of all France from the pages of Paul Bourget.

Fogazzaro attracts us by all those qualities in which his great rival is deficient. His outlook on life is wide and sane and sympathetic. He is a dreamer, and in his writing there is frequently a tinge of melancholy, inseparable from the capacity for dreaming; but his idealism is real and robust, and pervades all life within his vision, even to the horizon. I seem to feel that for him the colour of life must be mauve, pure and translucent, and a little chill. He has his full share of the spirit of patriotism, which has been a distinctive note of Italian literature during the present century. Italian unity was the dream of all romantic minds long before it became a political reality, and freedom from foreign despotism was felt to be an essential condition of intellectual achievement. In one respect at least, Fogazzaro is, as far as I know, unique among contemporary Italian writers. His sympathies, where they are not purely Italian, are Teutonic, and not French. His attitude is one of tacit protest against the preponderating influence of France in the intellectual life of his countrymen. For himself, he turns to Germany, and in the sentimentalism of the German character he discerns a wonderful charm. All through his books there are traces of his familiarity with the German literature of the present century, and there is no extravagance in the supposition that he has frequently derived inspiration from it. His very qualities are of a German order. His mind is refined, cultivated, a little deliberate. His work is never hurried; he observes carefully and sympathetically; and he reproduces with a detailed accuracy. But we must not seek in Fogazzaro's pages that passionate sense of beauty, that glow and warmth as of hot southern sunshine, which constitutes the irresistible attraction of D'Annunzio. To turn from one to the other is like passing from the luxurious boudoir of a woman of fashion to the bare simplicity of the convent parlour. Fogazzaro's feeling for his favourite Valsolda, which he has commemorated both in prose and verse, is rather one of quiet intimate affection—the affection of a lifetime—than a passionate identification of self with a scene of overmastering beauty. And so his descriptions of scenery, though we are conscious that they were felt by him, are not felt by us. We cannot realise the mountains that Franco and Luisa gazed upon from the *loggia* of their villa —although the author has described them to us a dozen times—as we realise the hillside clad in golden broom that stretched upwards behind the hermitage by the Adriatic where Giorgio and Ippolita sought in vain for happiness. The vivifying quality is absent.

Fogazzaro, on the other hand, possesses a considerable power of characterisation. There is perhaps a tendency in his portraits to caricature; he seizes, above all, the oddities in each individual, and dwells upon them with an indulgent satire. He seems to have laboured under the disadvantage of an admiration for Dickens. But he has presented his readers with a wide variety of types, each studied conscientiously, and, above all, he has shown something more than their mere surface distinctions. One of his greatest charms is his humanity. Nothing that affects the happiness of man is beneath his notice. He regards his neighbours with a benevolent and cordial philosophy; he penetrates their motives, and describes their actions in a spirit of kindly toleration, yet not without, here and there, the salt of a caustic wit. Note the tenderness with which, in the *Piccolo Mondo Antico*, he has drawn the ludicrous pathetic figure of 'La Pasotti'—her deafness, her terror of her husband, her unquenchable goodness of heart—making her lovable in spite of all her annoying absurdities, and contrast her with D'Annunzio's brutal picture of the old aunt Gioconda in the *Trionfo della Morte*. You see at a glance the fundamental difference between the pagan and the Christian outlook on life. It is not a question of insight—in both cases the women are drawn with a convincing reality, an elaboration of detail—it is a question of the attitude of the author towards human nature. D'Annunzio sees only the repulsive exterior, and turns aside, pitiless, his love of beauty outraged. Fogazzaro penetrates to the soul, and his own soul responds to the spiritual forces he discerns there.

It has been customary to speak of *Daniele Cortis* as being indisputably Fogazzaro's most remarkable work. In my opinion, it is in the *Piccolo Mondo Antico* that we see his talents in their most attractive development. The book is not without faults, but it is full of charm. It is long, but never wearisome. It should be read at leisure, in order that none of its delicate qualities may be overlooked. The *Piccolo Mondo Antico*, into which the author introduces his readers, is the 'little old world' of the Valsolda and other remote Alpine valleys lying round Lugano. It is a district into which, even to-day, the modern spirit of hurry and unrest has scarcely penetrated; and Fogazzaro's story carries us back to the middle of the century, to the last years of Austrian domination. Unfortunately, the dialogue is written in great measure in the special dialect of these southern slopes of the Alps, a bewildering mixture of French and Italian, which is almost incomprehensible to the foreigner. It is probably for this reason that the novel is so little known beyond the frontiers of Italy. It can hardly be read with full appreciation by any one who has not some previous acquaintance with local modes of speech. The author's own position in the matter has been adopted with full deliberation. He has laid it down as a literary precept that, whereas it is manifestly an error to make imaginary characters talk in pure Tuscan, without reference to the province from which they may come, it is equally a mistake to reproduce dialect—as Scott reproduced it—in all its native barbarity. A middle course must be chosen by which the genius of the dialect may be preserved without outrage to the cultured ear. His attitude is interesting in view of the fact that hitherto Tuscan alone has been considered worthy to rank as a written language, and the very efforts made to preserve its purity are responsible to a certain extent for the artificiality of the Italian literary language, which differs so widely from the vocabulary of daily speech. Manzoni, it will be remembered, did not make any of the characters in *I Promessi Sposi* speak in dialect ; but even Manzoni, as Dr. Garnett has reminded us in his *Italian Literature,* found it necessary to give his romance a thorough revision in order to bring its diction nearer to the Tuscan standard. There can be no doubt that his writing lost something of its natural vigour in the process. Fogazzaro's story gains, on the other hand, in vividness and individuality, and in a certain *bonhomie* which seems to spring from the rustic familiarity of his colloquial style, but it is not to be expected that his innovation should be popular among foreign readers.

Superficially, there is a noteworthy resemblance in sentiment between Manzoni and Fogazzaro. In their broad outlook on life, in patriotism, in religious faith, in intimate comprehension of the life of the Italian peasantry, they stand side by side. The Manzonian feeling is specially observable in *Piccolo Mondo Antico,* from the fact that it deals with the same Alpine district as *I Promessi Sposi*, and even a space of two hundred and fifty years brings but small changes to remote Italian villages. Yet in no sense can Fogazzaro be called an imitator of his great predecessor. His work is essentially his own, and in the field of fiction it covers many aspects of life on which Manzoni never touched. The story of *Piccolo Mondo Antico* is very simple; there is hardly any plot. In the opening chapter we learn that Don Franco Maironi, a young man of noble family, loves Luisa Rigey, a young girl of beauty and refinement, but his inferior in station. The marriage is celebrated in secret; Don Franco is disowned by his aristocratic grandmother; and the young couple take up their abode in an idyllic villa in the Valsolda with an uncle of the bride. The remainder of the book is concerned with the subtle influence of man and wife on each other, and of their environment on both. The time is in the stirring years between 1850 and 1860, when hatred of Austria in Lombardy and the Venetian provinces was at its height, and when a noble enthusiasm for freedom and unity inspired the Italian youth of the day. Don Franco has the artistic temperament, impulsive, enthusiastic, of quick sympathies, but lacking in energy and perseverance. He is gifted with a facile instinctive faith which accommodates itself easily to his daily habits, and allows him to follow his natural impulses, which are for the most part good. He dreams of liberty and national glory, and is content meanwhile to waste his life cultivating his garden under Austrian rule. Luisa is of much stronger mental fibre than her husband, much more intellectual, with an upright independent nature that clings to right and justice for their own sake, and to whom religious faith is not so much antagonistic as superfluous. The incompatibility of temperament of husband and wife soon shows itself. Franco is shocked by Luisa's freethinking tendencies, as well as secretly humiliated by her intellectual superiority, and Luisa is disedified by her husband's amiable inconsistencies of conduct. Even the little daughter Maria, to whom both are passionately attached, threatens to become a source of domestic discord. For myself, I regret that in a work whose great charm lies in its delicate appreciation of half-tones, in its deliberate portraiture of the little things, the little interests that go to make up the sum of life, a catastrophe so gratuitous and so violent as the drowning of the child should have been introduced merely as a means of bringing to a climax the relations between the parents. It is the volatile Franco with his optimistic nature and his firm faith in a future life who bears the trial best, and derives strength from it; whereas Luisa, who had evolved for herself a somewhat rationalistic conception of the world's justice, is crushed by what appears to her the horrible injustice of depriving her of her child. Husband and wife drift apart, and Luisa finds her only consolation in seeking for intercourse with her little daughter through spiritualistic media. In this latter portion of the story I am inclined to think the author has allowed his moral convictions to override his artistic perceptions. He feels that the believing husband ought to bear tribulation better than the unbelieving wife, and so he sets himself to prove that such was the case. But neither the despondency of Luisa nor the superior virtue of Franco is quite convincing. Neither the one nor the other is in entire harmony with our previous conceptions of the characters concerned. The transformation in Franco is too abrupt; and we feel that, quite apart from supernatural motives, Luisa's own nobility of character might have saved her from the morbid excesses of her grief. Happily, in the end her love for her husband is allowed to triumph over her despair, for her coldness is of the head and not of the heart, and the book closes on a charmingly conceived reconciliation on the eve of Franco's enrolment as a volunteer in the war against Austria. Knowing as we do that the author's personal sympathies are wholly on the side of his hero, it is pleasant to note the sympathetic understanding with which, in the earlier chapters at least, the personality of the heroine has been drawn. Unlike the conventional Italian women of romance, she is endowed with some measure at least of intellectual perception, and with an understanding of the undeveloped possibilities of life for her sex, outside the narrow circle of husband, and lover, and children. She is refined and high-principled, and the somewhat assertive element in her nature has in it no taint of masculinity. She is not without points of contact with Elena, the heroine of *Daniele Cortis*, but she is more interesting, more lovable, and will remain, I think, Fogazzaro's most successful feminine creation. Yet the fullest charm of the story lies neither in Franco nor yet in Luisa, but rather in the picture painted by Fogazzaro of the human society of his remote Alpine valley. If he fails in landscape drawing, he excels in conveying a sense of the atmosphere that envelops his characters. He sees all the poetry that permeates the lives of his circle of village card-players, of the petty little society of custom-house officers and attorneys and priests that clusters round the Marchesa Maironi. He has a keen appreciation of the monotonous sedentary life which is the normal fate of dwellers in these regions—nothing in all the book is more admirable than his long description of the tench-fishers sitting day after day in solitary contemplation over their rods round the lake—yet he is intensely sensitive to the vivifying effect of some breath from the great outer world which, from time to time, sweeps through the valleys. In his portrait of the benign old uncle Piero, indicated in a few slight touches, we are made conscious of a spiritual presence exercising a silent and beneficent influence on all who come within the radius of his vision. Piero symbolises the whole tendency of Fogazzaro's writing, which is to depict the modulating power of spiritual forces over the merely animal tendencies of human nature. All through *Piccolo Mondo Antico* there is no question of illicit passion—perhaps we have fallen here on the true explanation of its restricted popularity among novel-readers —yet no one can honestly assert that the author is in consequence less true to the facts of the life that he depicts. His idealism is of a quasi-religious character; it does not carry him up into heights from which the real conditions of life become invisible. But both he and his characters dwell in the pure bracing air of the mountain, and there is something of its crystalline quality between the covers of his book.

It was a conviction of the poverty of his country in the sphere of fiction, and of her entire dependence on foreign writers, that first moved the young poet, author of *Miranda*, a sentimental poetical tale, and of *Valsolda*, a collection of descriptive and lyrical verses, to turn his attention to romance. Lecturing at Vicenza in 1872, Fogazzaro had bewailed the necessity in which Italy found herself of begging the daily bread of fiction from foreign hands, and moreover of receiving from them bread which was not only unpalatable, but unwholesome. It was not till some years later that he himself entered the lists with his novel, *Malombra*, which excited at once an eager controversy among critics. Viewed in the light of his later work, it is surprising that this first effort should have called forth so much favourable notice; for its inferiority not only to *Piccolo Mondo Antico*, but also to *Daniele Cortis*, is immeasurable. The fact offers one more proof—if proof were needed—of the low ebb to which Italian literature had fallen some twenty years ago. The most obvious fault of *Malombra* is its amateurishness. It is not lacking in interest, and it gives evidence of unusual imaginative qualities, but it is unsatisfactory both in conception and execution. It is a medley of sentiments which the reader is never able to unravel. The author seems to have flung pell-mell into the book all the material at his disposal as though he were writing the one story of his lifetime, and were anxious to keep nothing back. There is no order, no sequence, no due sense of progression, and the reader, in spite of the well-maintained interest of the plot, grows weary and impatient. If, on the one hand, there is a love of melodramatic mystery in the conception of the gloomy castle by the lake, its ghost-haunted chambers and its eccentric owner, which recalls the Byronic ideals of the early century, we have, on the other, more strongly than in any of Fogazzaro's later works, evidences of purely Teutonic inspiration. It is clear that he had not, at that time, digested and assimilated the various influences which, in his later work, detract nothing from his originality, while giving to his writing the pleasant flavour of a refined culture. In opposition to his Italian heroine, Marina Crusnelli di Malombra, he has placed his German heroine, Edith, a typically serious and virtuous Teutonic maiden, and between the two vacillates his rather ineffectual literary hero Silla, whose reflections on life seem to suggest at times an autobiographical source. If passion draws Silla into the arms of Marina, love and gratitude lead him back to the feet of Edith. Curiously enough, the German Edith, as far as I am aware, is the only one of Fogazzaro's heroines that fulfils his ideal of feminine perfection. His own countrywomen appear to him rather as causes of temptation than as sources of inspiration. Luisa and Elena are both lacking in religious principle, and are only kept in the paths of virtue by the restraining influence respectively of Franco and of Cortis. And Marina, from the first, is clearly the Temptress incarnate. Marina lives in the haunted castle with her recluse uncle, and has already inveigled Silla into an anonymous literary correspondence before fate brings him to reside with her under her uncle's roof. Then she insults him, and the relations of the pair go through the conventional fluctuations of passion and loathing. Marina's ill-regulated mind has been rendered further unbalanced by the discovery of some relics of an insane grandmother who had been imprisoned in the castle for many years. Marina believes herself to be a re-incarnation of the mad Cecilia. She too, in the end, develops actual madness, and the novel ends with a sensational tragedy. It is in the climax that the main fault of the story lies. As a 'motif,' lunacy seems to me supremely inartistic in a romance; it is outside character, outside even of humanity, and once the insanity is established, the psychological interest is at an end. It should only be introduced—as in *Jane Eyre*—in its influence on the lives of others; the victim himself can never be other, from an artistic point of view, than an object of repulsion.

The only novel Fogazzaro has written which, strictly speaking, can be described as a *roman de mœurs* is *Daniele Cortis*, perhaps the best known of all his works. In it Fogazzaro has met the French novelists, so to speak, on their own ground. The theme is one that might have commended itself either to Bourget or to Daudet in his later years. Around the conventional situation of French fiction—a beautiful woman placed between her husband and her lover—the author has woven a study of Italian political life, of the official and financial society that clusters round Montecitorio. But the treatment of the theme differs fundamentally from that of his French contemporaries. From first to last the book is a protest against materialism, against the subjection of Will to Passion. In feeling it is purely idealist and sentimental. It is not fair to regard *Daniele Cortis* merely as an edifying tract, as a treatise in favour of the sanctity of the marriage tie—Fogazzaro is too accomplished an artist to thrust his moral down the throats of his readers—but it is undeniable that the book has a distinctly religious aim. In it the author has emphasised the principles which he has professed all through his literary career. He has put himself into direct opposition to the tendencies both of his time and his nation, tendencies of which D'Annunzio is the most able exponent, and to which Verga, Matilde Serao, de Roberti, and others have all subscribed. It is here that his main claim to distinction lies. It must have demanded no little courage to take up so *intransigeant* an attitude in moral questions, and to maintain it unflinchingly to the end. Even the sternest director of souls would have hesitated before banishing Elena to Yokohama with her husband under the circumstances. But the author never vacillates. If we feel—as I think the reader inevitably does feel—that throughout *Daniele Cortis* artistic considerations have been in a measure subordinated to what Fogazzaro has held to be the moral necessities of the case, it merely goes to prove that, charming and accomplished novelist as he is, he yet lacks the supreme artistic gift by which moral truths are rendered irresistibly convincing and beautiful to the average intelligence. We are all apt to be bored by the eternal verities instilled into us in our childhood. There is a superficial staleness about them which alienates our immediate sympathies. It is far easier for a novelist to excite interest on behalf of the transgressors, under special and plausible circumstances, of the great laws that bind Christian society, than to uphold convincingly the necessity for such laws. People's imaginations are fired much more quickly by the exceptional and accidental than by the normal and familiar. Half the secret of the popularity of fiction lies in this fact. It is only the supreme artists—Flaubert and Balzac, Turgenev and Tolstoi—who have declined to cater for man's superficial craving for entertainment, and who have painted humanity by the light of the great eternal truths of life. For their reward they have never attained to so-called 'popular' recognition. Fogazzaro can scarcely be numbered with one of these; yet, in virtue of the serious and honest purpose of his work, he may rightly claim our indulgence for faulty details of execution.

Although the central *motif* of the novel is the relation in which the heroine Elena stands to her husband, the Barone di Santa Giulia, on the one side, and to her cousin Daniele Cortis on the other, the author covers far wider ground than in the conventional *roman pas-*

sionnel. He possesses the art of introducing a great many minor motives into his picture without blurring the general effect. His talent for character drawing is displayed in the careful portrayal of the circle of worldly, gossiping, kind-hearted friends, who surround Elena and her mother, but he scarcely seems to me as happy as in his delineation of humbler folk. Then there is a study of Elena's uncle Lao, a somewhal original type of hypochondriac, who can forget his ailments sufficiently to cultivate a very chivalrous devotion to his unhappy niece. There is a charm and a sincerity in the affection that binds uncle and niece which are somehow lacking in the relations between Elena and her cousin. Cortis is a rising politician, a member of the Italian Chamber, and a good deal of space is given to his political views and to the parliamentary situation of the moment. It comes almost with a shock of surprise to find politics and social subjects even mentioned in an Italian novel. We gather that Cortis has democratic tendencies, and that his political sympathies are with the small body of Liberal Catholics whose organ is the *Ras-*

segna Nazionale. He is represented as the type of man, rare in real life in Italy, and rarer still in fiction, who does not allow his career to be dominated by the passion of the moment. In the midst of his love for Elena he remembers the claims of his constituents; and when he loses her for ever, he telegraphs to his supporters in Rome that he is entirely at their service. It is very praiseworthy no doubt, but somehow we cannot feel attracted by the man. There is in Cortis, as in many admirable people in real life, a touch of the prig. Honest and upright he may be, but he is also self-righteous. All through the book he makes discreet love to his married cousin, deceiving both himself and her as to whither they are tending; yet when the crisis is reached, it is with an almost unctuous virtue that he recalls her to a sense of her conjugal duty. Perhaps the only occasion when we can really feel for him is in the first scene between him and his mother at Lugano —he, cold, tortured, dignified; she, hypocritically pathetic. Madame Cortis had left her husband a few years after Daniele's birth, and her son had always believed her to be dead.

the young politician, driven to visit her by a sense of filial duty, finds her living under squalid and suspicious circumstances in a fifth-rate villa. The scene is admirable—no doubt one of those which caused the Italian critic Nencioni to declare that Fogazzaro's real talents lay in the direction of the drama. His dialogue at such times is commendably crisp and vigorous, and in the merely technical qualities of his work he has made palpable progress since the days when he wrote *Malombra*. Perhaps his more recent tendency is to put too stern a restraint upon himself. The style of *Daniele Cortis* is singularly reticent and chill, almost dry. In his latest novel Fogazzaro scarcely ever describes; he merely relates. Even Rome, strange to say, excites no emotions within him, and although it is the scene of a large portion of his story, he vouchsafes scarcely a line to the Eternal City. His heroine Elena is not very heroic, nor is she particularly attractive by her qualities, but she possesses the charm of her intense femininity. All through the book she vacillates between her sense of duty on the one side, and her love for undeniable that the greater portion of human life is spent in a chronic state of vacillation, in a vain effort after a workable compromise, we are apt to demand in our fiction that the characters should be above all things logical. No one is logical in real life, yet a semblance of logic seems essential in order to give reality to an imaginary personage. It says much for the author's skill in portraiture, and for his discernment of the true forces that go to make up character, that his helpless, storm-tossed heroine should be as real and comprehensible as she is. In the end Elena acts in accordance with the author's idealistic conception of conjugal duty. She has a feminine capacity for self-sacrifice, and having deliberately sacrificed her own happiness, together with that of Cortis and of her uncle, she sails for Yokohama with her husband, who has never made any secret of his indifference to her person. With her departure Fogazzaro wisely brings his story to a close—he would surely have had to repent of his idealism had he been obliged to record the havoc it must have wrought in this prosaic world in the lives of all concerned.

To read the novels of Antonio Fogazzaro and Gabriele D'Annunzio is to read the best that Italian fiction can offer in two opposing realms of thought. The two men stand poles asunder—between them lies the whole field of contemporary Italian literature. I will not attempt to weigh their merits in the balance; nor will I attempt the yet more futile task of foretelling their influence on the literary future of their country. What is essential is to realise that they are the latest expression of unchanging forces in the national life of Italy. They counteract and complement one another; they can never be assimilated. To-day paganism is triumphant in art, as it was triumphant in the days of the Renaissance, and the most skilled artificers in painting, in poetry, in music are drawn within the radius of its potent fascinations. But for those of us who love Chartres Cathedral and Fra Angelico, the *Divina Commedia*, and the *Imitation of Christ*, the old taunt that Christian Faith is destructive of true art can bear no meaning, and we are content to wait until the swing of the pendulum shall be set in the opposite direction.

HENRYK SIENKIEWICZ

In attempting to form a critical estimate of a foreign writer, there is nothing so difficult as to arrive at any just appreciation of his position in relation to the literary development of his own country. We are apt, from sheer ignorance, to regard him too exclusively from the standpoint of our own literary ideals, and not sufficiently from that of the country to which he belongs. Too often he appears to us, gazing from afar, as a solitary shining star, when in reality he is but one of a cluster of constellations. Every one will admit, in principle, that some considerable knowledge of the language, the literature, the history, the popular characteristics of a nation is needful, before a fair estimate of any individual author can be arrived at. And yet we are all of us guilty at times of basing our assertions on the most slender stock of general information. For every thousand persons who read the plays of Henrik Ibsen with a certain measure of intelligent appreciation, and pronounce judgment upon him with an assumption of dogmatic infallibility, there is probably scarcely one who could give the barest outline of the history of Scandinavian literature even during the present century; certainly not one who can read the dramatist in the original. True, if we refrained from expressing an opinion concerning foreign writers until we knew as much as, let us say, Taine knew of England before he wrote his *History of English Literature*, or, we may fairly add, as Dr. Garnett knows of Italian literature to-day, we should most of us be silent for a lifetime. But it is at least becoming and wholesome to remember our limitations, and to bear in mind that at best our criticisms are apt to be hasty and one-sided and spasmodic, and that they run great risk of being gravely deficient in a sense of proportion.

This is specially the case when we come to deal with Slav literature. For the nations of Western Europe the great Slav race is still, in a sense, enveloped in mystery. In faith, in history, in temperament, its people are far removed from ourselves. Their ideals differ widely from our own; their future contains the promise of boundless possibilities, which as a rival race we do not always contemplate with equanimity; and their life, as it stands revealed to us by their literature, impresses us mainly with a sense of its remoteness, almost of its unreality. It is this very mystery which gives to Slav literature a portion of its charm in the eyes of Western readers. Through its pages we learn to realise—partially, no doubt, and without due proportion—a race, dreamy, emotional, idealistic, full of a passionate faith and patriotism, not wholly emancipated from Asiatic fatalism, and with an under-current of melancholy, which, brought into contact with Western civilisation, frequently changes to blackest pessimism and unbelief. A deep chasm, that no bridge can span, seems to separate the Slav from the sturdy Teuton, from the sensual, concrete Latin. Tolstoi and Turgenev, Gogol and Dostoievsky have indeed revealed much to us, and more may be learned from the marvellous treasures of Slav folk-lore, which are being gathered together by patient labour, and brought within the reach even of English readers. And yet for me there will always remain some subtle, intangible element in Slav nature which penetrates through Slav literature, some elusive quality which seems to defy the intelligence of the Western critic and to render abortive all efforts to grasp in its entirety the spirit of the race.

Something of this intangibility envelopes the personality of Henryk Sienkiewicz. He is not only a Slav, but a Pole, and within the wide circle of the Slav nations the Poles have many characteristics of their own. They alone form a Catholic community in the midst of orthodox environment. They alone, the first of the Slav nations to emerge from barbarism and to embrace Christianity, have fallen back in the midst of that great uprising and spreading of the Slav race which constitutes one of the greatest historical facts of the nineteenth century. The possessors of many attractive qualities, the Poles have shown themselves singularly lacking in the gift of self-government. Unprotected by any natural boundaries, they have long ceased to represent a political or geographical entity. And yet the Polish nation still lives; its language survives, and it can claim to possess an art and a literature illustrative of its highest aspirations. To-day its most distinguished representative is the novelist, Henryk Sienkiewicz. He may be accepted in a sense as the type of the modern intellectual Pole. By birth and by education a Catholic, an aristocrat and a conservative, he has not wholly escaped the intellectual scepticism of our time. A great traveller, a student of social conditions under many and varied circumstances, his mental attitude is that of an onlooker rather than of an actor in life. He has no philosophy to propound, no convictions to preach; with his own mind in a state of suspense, he works as a painter rather than as a teacher and writer. In spite of his remarkable abilities, amounting almost to genius, and his undoubted industry, there is not a little of the dilettante in his attitude towards life; but the attitude is perhaps rather an intellectual pose than the outcome of the limitations of his nature. To a keen sense of the beautiful and a luxuriant and romantic imagination he adds a true and sympathetic appreciation of peasant life. Yet he is in no sense a democrat. His sympathy is that of the artist who sees the beauty of simple, laborious lives and the pathos of silent suffering. If in his writings he has glorified both the noble and the peasant, it is because his own nation appeals to him more vividly than any other, and the Polish people consists mainly of an exclusive and inefficient aristocracy and a vast, inarticulate peasantry. To their faults and their failings, as well as to their sterling qualities and their pervading charm, he has shown himself uniformly sensitive.

It was by his short stories and his studies of peasant life that Sienkiewicz first made his reputation in Poland. Unfortunately, in their very slightness of form and their delicate felicity of language, they present special difficulties to the translator; and Mr. Jeremiah Curtin, in spite of all his enthusiasm for his author, cannot be said to have carried out his task in an adequate manner. In his passion for literalness his version is frequently obscure, and his phrases rough and unpolished. Hence, without any acquaintance with the Polish language, it is impossible to express more than a tentative opinion concerning these essentially national studies. Polish critics have lavished what to English readers must seem almost extravagant praise upon their truth, their pathos, their marvellous insight into the life of the people. I must confess that the strange, weird little tale, *Yanko the Musician*, over which all Poland sobbed and raved when it was first published, some twenty years ago, disappointed me not a little. I am perhaps hard-hearted enough to think that the pathos of childhood has been considerably overdone in modern literature. And our power of sympathy being, after all, very limited, this story of a poor, little, half-witted peasant child is perhaps too remote from our ordinary English experience to touch us in any very convincing fashion. The language, moreover, has been robbed by translation of well nigh all its beauty. Yet all who would learn to penetrate into the life of the Polish people, to fathom something of Slav nature in its primitive simplicity, will find much that is suggestive in the short sketches which in the English version have been gathered together in the volumes entitled *Yanko the Musician* and *Hania*. In their rather obvious pathos, their quick sympathy with humble joys and sorrows, and their tone here and there of humorous scepticism, they have not a little in common with Alphonse Daudet's early *contes*, the *Lettres de mon Moulin*. As we read such tales as *Bartek the Victor* or *The Organist of Ponikla* the Polish peasant seems to emerge before us from his obscurity and take on real flesh and blood. But Sienkiewicz is capable of striking a far deeper note than Daudet reveals. In *Charcoal Studies*, perhaps the most famous of his shorter works, in the story of the downfall of Repa and his wife, there is all the tragedy of a great drama hidden away beneath sordid circumstance. Sienkiewicz is intensely sensitive to the passion of inarticulate grief; but, with true artistic sense, he restrains himself in these tales of peasant life within the limits of a simple, unadorned narrative. Here is a word-picture of the woman returning home after a futile effort to intercede with the authorities on behalf of her husband. There is a haunting quality in the scene :—

'But Repa's wife? Peasants when they suffer merely suffer, nothing more. This woman in the strong hand of misfortune was simply like a bird tormented by a vicious child. She went forward; the wind drove her; sweat flowed from her forehead; and that was the whole history. At times, when the child who was sick opened his mouth and began to pant, as if ready to die, she called to him, " Yasek, Oh Yasek, my heart!" And she pressed her lips of a mother to the heated forehead of the little one. She passed the pre-Reformation Church, and went on into the field till she stopped on a sudden—a drunken peasant was coming toward her.'

As a historical novelist it is not possible to classify Sienkiewicz in any school. By his luxuriant imagination, his buoyant optimism, and by the faith, the patriotism, and the love of chivalry that illuminate his pages, he belongs to the romantics. But he is a realist in the veracity of his descriptions, in the grim reality of his battle scenes, and in his relentless pictures of war and all its attendant horrors. With all his patriotism he is never blind to Polish faults. In his great historical trilogy,[1] the outcome of eight years' labour, he shows us Polish nature at its best—idealistic, passionately patriotic, instinct with Catholic faith, splendidly courageous, yet at the same time petty, unreliable, jealous, and somehow accomplishing little of permanent value. He deals with one of the most critical periods in Polish history— the latter half of the seventeenth century— when Poland was assailed in turn by Cossack and Tartar, by Turk and Swede, a period at once of crushing blows and splendid victories. Yet with all the fighting and fury, all the faith and patriotism of these years, they lead up inevitably to Poland's final defeat and ultimate partition. Sienkiewicz himself is haunted by a sense of what in another novel he has termed 'l'improductivité Slave.' It is clear to writer and reader alike that something essential is lacking in this charming, emotional, inconsequent people; and the sense of this lack, in

[1] *With Fire and Sword*, 1 vol.; *The Deluge*, 2 vols.; *Pan Michael*, 1 vol.

which in a measure Sienkiewicz feels himself to participate, gives an under-currrent of melancholy to all his writing.

There is nothing conventional in his treatment of historical themes. He has created a veritable Round Table of famous knights, each with his special characteristics and his long roll of doughty deeds: the terrible Kmita and Pan Michael, surnamed 'the little knight,' the Falstaffian Zagloba, the soldier-prior Kordetski, and the pious Pan Longin, who dies like St. Sebastian. In Azya and in Bogun we have types of Cossack ferocity and cunning, and above these imaginary characters there tower the great historical figures, drawn in bold, effective outline: John Sobieski, the saviour of his country and of Europe; the Russian leader Hmelnitski, who worked such ruin for Poland; the saintly king Yan Kasimir; and the arch-traitor Prince Radziwill, who intrigued with Sweden against his country's independence. Sienkiewicz's heroes are real flesh and blood, men of wild courage and unrestrained passions, capable at once of heroic self-sacrifice and of the most implacable vengeance. They do not effect miraculous escapes from every danger according to the approved methods of heroes of romance; rather, they die the death of valiant warriors on the battlefield. And their women-folk, whether they be stately and tender-hearted as Olenka, the heroine of *The Deluge*, or intrepid and impulsive as Basia, the fitting wife of Pan Michael, follow their husbands in camp or fortress, and share to the full in the fortunes of war, even to being sold as slaves into Turkish harems, the worst of all fates that awaited the Christian women of those regions in moments of defeat. Sienkiewicz never falls into the snare of putting nineteenth century sentiments on to seventeenth century lips. There was no pity in those days either for heretics or traitors, and the author shows none. Even after his conversion, Kmita, the wild hero of *The Deluge*, puts his enemy Kuklinovski to a slow and horrible death, and gloats over his sufferings, and rides away content, with a prayer on his lips. He ruthlessly lets loose his Tartar hordes on unoffending German and Protestant villages to slay and plunder to their full, though for long months he had held them in check from touching a Catholic or a Pole. And he repeats his *Aves* in the midst of the slaughter, feeling that he is doing the Lord's work. It is difficult, with our highly developed humanitarianism, to put ourselves in this frame of mind. That the author should have done so is a testimony to his skill as a writer of romance; for I have not the smallest doubt that it is absolutely true to the times of which he is writing. Probably also, in spite of Tolstoi's propaganda of the doctrine of non-resistance to evil, the principles of universal toleration are not as yet very widely diffused throughout the countries of Eastern Europe.

The Deluge, in spite of its really inordinate length, is the most spirited and the most engrossing of the historical tales. The book opens with a charming picture of Olenka, the heroine, sitting among her spinning maidens in her ancestral home—a picture of peace—then all the rest of the book tells of war and adventure. Briefly put, it recounts the invasion of Poland by Charles Gustavus of Sweden, the treachery of some of the Polish nobles, and the final expulsion of the Swedes through a great uprising of the whole nation in defence of their land and their faith. When Poland already lay prostrate beneath the Swedish heel, the invaders, in an evil moment for themselves, decided to occupy the great shrine of Our Lady of Chenstohova in the fortress-church of Yasna Gora. At once Polish faith was aflame; devotion to the shrine effected what even patriotism had failed to accomplish; and the almost miraculous defence of the fortress-church against overwhelming odds proved the turning-point in the war. The chapters telling of the siege are written with a splendid spirit and enthusiasm. For once the author has abandoned his half-critical, half-sceptical attitude towards life, and has allowed himself to be carried away by the romance of his subject. He writes in the fullest sympathy with the robust Catholic faith of his forefathers. In this connection it is possible to draw a very instructive parallel between the attitude of mind of the Polish novelist and that of two contemporary writers of fiction—Zola and Gabriele D'Annunzio. All three have described a popular pilgrimage to a shrine of the Blessed Virgin—Zola in *Lourdes,* D'Annunzio in what I can only describe as a singularly repulsive chapter of the *Trionfo della Morte,* and Sienkiewicz in *The Deluge.* In all three cases the external facts are absolutely identical; we have the same crowds of the poor and the afflicted, the same frenzy of devotion concentrated upon a wonder-working shrine. But whereas the two Latin authors can see nothing but what is gross and repulsive in the merely physical aspects of the phenomenon, the Slav writer sees the same facts in all their spiritual significance, transformed and illuminated by faith. Materialism has not penetrated into Poland, and Sienkiewicz puts on human actions their natural interpretation, instead of distorting them, as is the fashion among the disciples of the so-called naturalist school, into illustrations of their own narrow and perverted theories.

In *Without Dogma* we are transported into a very different world. Rightly, I think, it has been accepted as the author's ablest work, and to many the subject will appeal as one of engrossing interest. On me, I confess, the book, with all its brilliant cleverness, made a somewhat melancholy impression. It is the history of a modern sceptic without faith or morals, a man incapable of action, morbid, egotistic, pitiless to others, but with marvellously acute sensibilities. He is, in a word, a Slav version of D'Annunzio's decadent Italian heroes. Leo Ploszowski, who relates the story in the first person, has been accepted without much justification as a portrait of the novelist himself—certainly a malicious one, for Ploszowski is described as rendered sterile through scepticism, cursed with what he himself has termed 'l'improductivité Slave,' whereas Sienkiewicz has justified his life by his work. Portrait or no portrait, the author has clearly intended to unite in the person of his hero the opposing elements which have gone to build up his own life. Ploszowski stands midway between Paganism and Christianity, attracted and repelled in turn by one and the other. To the beauties of both he is acutely sensitive; the ultimate choice is never made. The dilemma, at once ethical, intellectual, and æsthetic, possesses a singular, and doubtless a personal fascination for the Polish novelist; for, under altered conditions, it forms the groundwork of his Roman story, *Quo Vadis*. Ploszowski is merely the modern equivalent of Petronius. Petronius was the most exquisite product of the dying pagan world brought into contact with nascent Christianity; Ploszowski is the latest product of a recrudescent paganism, ready to spring up wherever the Christian ideal has grown faint. The conflict between the flesh and the spirit, between paganism and faith, between the philosophy of beauty and the doctrines of Christ, is in all essentials the same, whether the battlefield be modern Europe or ancient Rome. And yet, happily, eighteen centuries of Christianity cannot be flung off by the mere wish; Christian ethics have penetrated too deeply into our consciences through many generations. We cannot, if we would, put ourselves wholly back into the spirit of ancient Hellas. At its best the attempt is but a pose, a graceful affectation, which does not really correspond to the inmost needs of our modern natures. At its worst it is a mere cloak for sensual materialism. Sienkiewicz has put this truth into words that seem to me worth quoting, for they show that he himself has never been wholly carried away by the specious arguments which he places on the lips of his hero.

'It seems to me,' he writes, 'that a Christian soul, though the spring of faith be dried up within him, cannot live altogether on the mere beauty of form. . . . We are beings of a different culture. Our souls are full of Gothic arches, pinnacles, twisted traceries that we cannot shake off, and of which Greek minds knew nothing. Our minds shoot upward; theirs, full of repose and simplicity, rested nearer the earth. Those of us in whom the spirit of Hellas beats more powerfully, consider the beautiful a necessity of life, and search after it eagerly, but they instinctively demand that Aspasia should have the eyes of Dante's Beatrice. A similar longing is planted within me. When I think of it, that a beautiful human animal like Laura belongs to me, and will belong as long as I wish it, a twofold joy gets hold of me—the joy of the man and the delight of the artist; and yet there is a want, a something missing. On the altar of my

Greek temple there is a marble goddess ; but my Gothic shrine is empty.'

If the author has given to paganism the ascendency in the case of Ploszowski, he has caused Christianity to triumph in the person of the hero's cousin Aniela. Briefly, the book is the history of the spiritual combat between the two. A marriage has been arranged between them by their respective families, and Aniela has already betrayed her readiness to be wooed, when, impelled partly by circumstances, partly by his own indolent egotism and by a temporary enslavement to a beautiful American in Rome, Ploszowski rejects the proposed alliance in an insulting manner. Aniela, for financial and family reasons, marries a man quite unworthy of her, and immediately the dormant passion in Ploszowski awakes, and he hurries back to his ancestral home with the deliberate purpose of overcoming Aniela's scruples and winning her for himself. The cousinship, the temporary absence of the husband, and the fact that Aniela as the guest of his aunt is living under his own roof, give him every advantage of circumstance. But the weapons on which he mainly relies in his cold-blooded scheme are his own intellectual superiority, and an assumption of a wider moral understanding and enfranchisement from antiquated superstitions. It is a situation that has been frequently depicted in modern French fiction, but, as a rule, with an entirely different *dénouement*. The comparison is interesting as emphasising one of the many points of difference between the ethical ideals of the Slav and the Latin races. According to the contemporary French novelist—to M. Bourget, let us say—Aniela would have been compelled to yield to Ploszowski as to some superior force; his worldly philosophy and his somewhat hollow protestations would have triumphed over her scruples, for the simple reason that there would have been nothing in her nature capable of opposing an inflexible resistance. It would be inconceivable to M. Bourget and his school that a beautiful woman could resist. Sienkiewicz, who treats the situation not only with exceeding elaboration of detail, but with an almost painful familiarity with the baser workings of a man's perverted imagination, approaches his heroine from an entirely different standpoint. He belongs to a nation whose women have been as celebrated for their faith and their virtue as for their personal charms; and if he insists, as he has insisted, on the force of the temptation; if he has provided Aniela with every worldly excuse for giving herself to the man she has always loved, it is only to bring out more emphatically the strength of her powers of resistance. He is conscious all through—and the thoughtful reader is conscious with him—that, being the woman she is, Aniela can never yield. All Ploszowski's specious arguments, all his eloquence, all his intellectual superiority fall to the ground before Aniela's simple statement: 'Everything may be proved in some way or other; but when we do wrong, our conscience tells us, "It is wrong, wrong," and nothing can convince it to the contrary.' Conscience is invincible. The story ends with the entry, 'Aniela died this morning.' And Aniela's resistance is frankly founded by the author on her religious faith, on the invincible strength of purity which Christianity alone has developed, but which does exist to-day in the normally constituted woman. It is one of those essential truths which modern novelists, with all their boasted psychology, have lost sight of. Aniela is a type: M. Bourget's women remain abnormal exceptions. And what I have said of the heroine of *Without Dogma* is true of well nigh all Sienkiewicz's heroines. We escape entirely in his books from the neurotic, hysterical women who have been allowed to hold the field unchallenged in much recent fiction, and still more in recent drama. Sceptic as Sienkiewicz frequently shows himself, he has no scepticism where women are concerned. His female characters are all heathy, normal women, neither prudes nor wantons, women of warm hearts and simple, strong passions, and generally of unswerving fidelity. It is probably fair to assume that he has painted them as, in the main, he has known them in his own country, and his experience has not been without influence on his whole attitude towards life. I emphasise the point, as it has been customary to identify his views in every particular with those of Ploszowski rather than with those of Aniela. I think myself they must be identified with neither; rather both extremes indicate the two points between which the pendulum of his mind swings. He writes, as I have said, with his mind in suspense, and he seldom takes upon himself the duty of pointing a definite moral.

Quo Vadis is the only one of Sienkiewicz's books with a clearly didactic aim, and artistically it has suffered not a little from the fact. Nevertheless, it is by *Quo Vadis* that his European—as distinct from his Polish—reputation has mainly been made. Stories of early Christian times have, not unnaturally, always enjoyed a wide popularity. The planting of Christianity in Rome, and the final absorption of the great Roman Empire within the Christian commonwealth, is probably the most stupendous fact in all history. Hence it is not surprising that Sienkiewicz's novel, dealing, not without considerable power, with some of the momentous years of the struggle, should have carried his reputation through Europe far more quickly than any of his previous romances. Written but a couple of years ago, it has already been translated into almost every

European language. Nevertheless, I should not for a moment put *Quo Vadis* on the same literary level as *Without Dogma*, or as some of the early Polish tales. It is in the main a study of mere exteriority; it is a rich mosaic elaborately pieced together bit by bit. Written after much conscientious research, it lacks as a romance both grace and spontaneity. It contains little characterisation, and very little of that sympathetic identification of the author with his subject which constitutes one of the main charms of his national romances. Sienkiewicz has himself been overburdened at times with his own learning, and having laboriously acquired it, he has not had the fortitude to deny himself the pleasure of inflicting it on his readers. It was impossible for him to fling himself into the life of the ancient Romans with the verve and energy with which he treats of the Polish heroes who were his own direct ancestors. Moreover, the modern world is so impressed with the stateliness of the Roman character, that it is singularly difficult for us to realise the *civis romanus* in his moments of ease and mirth. All this necessarily militates against the success of the book as a work of art. But with these limitations I am ready to admit that much of the story is exceedingly interesting. For all who love Rome of the present day, the resuscitation beneath the hand of the novelist of the ancient city, of which to-day we can only see a few glorious fragments, possesses a wonderful charm. One would give a great deal to view the busy Forum, the stately crowds passing to and from the Capitol, the undimmed glory of the temples which rise before one's mental vision as one peruses Sienkiewicz's pages. He has chosen as the moment of his story the reign of Nero with all its excesses and debauchery, and the arrival of St. Peter and St. Paul in the city. As in *Without Dogma*, he has sought his effects in strong contrasts placed side by side. On the one hand tyranny and violence, lust and luxury, the grimly grotesque figure of Nero looming over all; on the other, meekness and longsuffering and the teachings of Christ. The decadence of Rome heralds the dawn of modern Europe. There is no glossing over the state of Roman society in the first century.

Sienkiewicz grapples with it boldly, and without unduly emphasising gross details, the facts are plainly stated with all the honesty which is one of his greatest merits. Without the early chapters, describing in luxuriant detail the magnificence of the Roman palaces and the wild orgies that took place in them, the reader could not have appreciated the full horror of the burning of the city, and the subsequent persecution of the Christians. Without the pagan love of Petronius for Eunice, he would not have perceived so clearly the spiritual bond that united Vinicius to Lygia. It is characteristic of our author that of all the personages he introduces, it is Petronius alone who seems to appeal to him, and who, consequently, appeals also to us. Petronius, the man of the world, the *arbiter elegantiarum* of his day, the most exquisite type of refined paganism, a lifelong worshipper of beauty, nevertheless wavers before Christianity, and dimly perceives its mysterious power, and thus he is brought within the sphere of our nineteenth century sympathies. For the rest, Lygia is the conventional Christian maiden of fiction, whose fate it is to be saved from the lions, and no one else stands out from the crowded picture with any distinctness.

These three series of books taken together —the historical romances, *Quo Vadis* and *Without Dogma*—show the broad sweep of Sienkiewicz's talents. He has not only done admirable work, but he has done a great deal of it. I have not touched on the innumerable descriptions of nature scattered through his pages, which are held by his countrymen to constitute one of his highest claims to fame, because it is impossible to judge of them adequately in the only translations we possess. But all can appreciate his skill in human portraiture. He has created a veritable picture gallery, not only of Polish knights and ladies, but of men and women in every rank of life, who stand out from the canvas in clear, crisp outline. He has made the silent, inarticulate Polish peasant human and comprehensible to readers living thousands of miles away. As a story-teller, pure and simple, he deserves very high rank. And the atmosphere of his books is, in the main, pure and wholesome. He has escaped all contact with the naturalist school of

France—already, happily, a thing of the past —and in an age when an assumption of cosmopolitanism has come to be regarded as a proof of superior culture in writers of fiction he has had the courage to remain frankly Polish in his sympathies and predilections. His weakness lies in the tinge of dilettantism that infects much of his work. His attitude towards life is tentative and uncertain; he has never frankly taken up a position either on one side or the other. If his books have gained in elaborateness of analysis and in a sympathetic appreciation of life under very varying aspects, they have certainly lost in robustness and vigour. Undoubtedly, the strongest and truest emotion of which Sienkiewicz is capable is his patriotism, and it is by his patriotism that he will live. He has written of life in all ages and in many lands, but I venture to think it is only on Polish soil and dealing with Polish nature that he can claim to be an artist of the first rank. It will not be as the author of *Quo Vadis*, but rather as the interpreter of the genius and the aspirations of a now vanished nation, that his name will be honoured in the future.

WAR AND PEACE

WHEN Tolstoi wrote *War and Peace*, he wrote the great prose epic of the nineteenth century. It is only from Russia that such an epic could come. It is only the Slav race that in our own day could provide the material for a work at once so vast in its proportions and so heroic in its incidents. *War and Peace* presents all the characteristics of the true epic; it is an imaginative work based on a great national upheaval, permeated by an intense patriotism. It is something much more than an historical romance. It has given voice to a national ideal, and it has placed on permanent record in a popular form the deeds of valour on which the power of an Empire is based. Tolstoi has celebrated the first emergence of his country from Asiatic barbarism, the first entry of the great Slav Empire into the conclave of European nations. He has painted a war which in magnitude both actual and potential far outweighs any other war of modern times, and he has painted it in all its far-reaching effects on the life and development of the people, in all its spiritual significance. And this history of his nation is typified in the life-history of a number of imaginary personages, men and women so real and so human, that they break down the barriers that divide race from race, and render intelligible to the outside world a national life of strongly marked characteristics. Surely in such a scheme there is something little short of Homeric.

War and Peace, though it occupied many years in writing, belongs in its entirety to the earlier portion of the novelist's career. The first chapters appeared in serial form in 1865, and it was ten years later before he published his second great novel, *Anna Karenina*. The period of composition coincided with years of doubt, and inquiry, and mental growth in the life of the author, years that led up to the final evolution of his later philosophy of life, the philosophy founded on the words, 'Resist not Evil.' Towards the close of his epic there are indications that his theories have taken on a more definite shape, but throughout the greater part of the work they exist only in a latent condition. They give colour and atmosphere to his pictures and life; they give vigour to his grasp of social problems, but they are subordinate to the artistic intention. In *War and Peace* Tolstoi writes as an artist, not as a teacher, whereas since the publication of *Anna Karenina* he has written as a teacher, and his artistic gifts have been subordinate to his moral aims. We have heard so much of late years of the Count in his *rôle* of reformer and moralist and preacher of a new Christianity, that we are apt to forget that he is also, and indeed primarily, a great artist. *War and Peace*, like *Anna Karenina*, is, above all, a superb work of art, and it is surely worth while putting aside for the moment those philosophic considerations that spring from his writings to inquire into the special gifts of perception and style and construction which entitle him to a foremost place among the imaginative writers of the century.

It is customary to place *War and Peace* as a work of art on a lower level than its successor. In reality, no comparison is possible between them. *Anna Karenina* takes undisputed rank among the half-dozen greatest novels of the century. *War and Peace* must be judged by an entirely different standard. The very title itself—unless we accept it as a presumptuous misnomer—is a guarantee that the book is something more than a *roman de mœurs*. If we once accept the view that it is an epic and not a novel, the main accusation brought against it, its inordinate length, falls to the ground. For an epic is of necessity long. *The Iliad*, *The Æneid*, *The Divina Commedia*, are all of exceeding length. True, in *War and Peace* there are certain *longueurs* with which all but the most enthusiastic disciples of Tolstoi would gladly dispense, pages of philosophy, most of which are omitted in the French translation, and descriptive interludes such as the hunting episodes at Otradnoë, which do not help forward the story in any appreciable manner. Yet bearing in mind the vast scope of the enterprise—the presentment of a great nation in war-time and in peace—there are few scenes which do not complete in one direction or another the author's scheme.

Again, we can dispense with unity of interest more easily in a prose epic than in a novel, although it must be admitted that the greatest of novelists have frequently selected the widest canvases for their themes, and that Tolstoi himself in *Anna Karenina* has given us concurrently two threads of interest, with no necessary connection between them, in the love story, on the one hand, of Vronski and Anna, and on the other of Levine and Kitty. An epic gives us a certain march of events seen both in their general effects and in their individual application. This is precisely what Tolstoi has done in *War and Peace*. There is no plot properly so called. He takes us from the drawing-room to the battlefield, and back again to the peaceful routine of country-house life. He conducts us through several campaigns, and shows how in the brief intervals of peace the nation returned with avidity to its normal occupations. The history of the various characters introduced is closely interwoven with the course of public affairs ; each is treated in turn. Thus the reader roams necessarily over an exceedingly wide field. There are centres of interest in different parts of the Russian Empire, bound together by very slender threads; there is the circle of society at Moscow and the circle at St. Petersburg; there are at least three heroes, Pierre Besukov, Nicolas Rostov, and Prince André; and if there is but one heroine, Natasha —for who can approach Natasha in interest?— there are several other ladies, Sonia, Elena Besukov, and the Princess Marie, who each claim a considerable share of our attention. Side by side with the fictitious characters there is a long list of historical personages—the Emperor and his entourage and all the generals and aides-de-camp who figure in the campaign. This numerous company is handled by the author with an amazing freedom and sureness of touch. Each one is endowed with an individual humanity, with an elaborate network of qualities and emotions, the threads of which are never allowed to tangle. Nothing could be more admirable in technique than the opening chapter in which the elegant crowd that thronged the salons of Anna Pavlovna at her evening party is introduced to the reader. The inane futility of society gossip is laid bare, but it is done without a sneer, with a wide toleration and comprehension of human frailty. I cannot refrain from contrasting the scene with the presentment of society given to us recently in *The Ambassador*. In Mrs. Craigie's play but a single motive, social jealousy, inspires the whole of the dialogue, which quickly wearies by the automatic brilliancy of the repartee and the monotony of the type presented. In Tolstoi's dialogue, under practically identical circumstances, the identity of every speaker is preserved in the delicate give-and-take of refined social intercourse, and the cross currents of love, jealousy, vanity, curiosity, each find a place.

The trait which more than any other seems to me to distinguish Tolstoi from the successful French novelists of the day is, that whereas their first effort is to explain their characters to their readers, to make them logical, to account for all their actions, Tolstoi realises from the first that human nature can never be explained in its entirety; that behind all that can be seen and accounted for there lie unseen forces which may act at times with volcanic results. He realises that every human soul is to a great extent, to the outside world, a *terra incognita*, that it is wrapped in mystery, that the element of certainty in respect to it is in very small proportion to the element of uncertainty. It is just because Tolstoi professes to understand so much less than the average novelist that we know that he understands so much more; he does not attempt the impossible, but he throws flashes of light into the prevailing darkness; and what he reveals to us, he reveals with all the more convincing effect because of the surrounding gloom.

What is true of his character-drawing is equally true of his pictures of war. The ordinary military historian is ready to point out how every operation, every manœuvre, is the result of some carefully prepared plan. He reduces the science of war to a mathematical calculation, and affects at least to believe that a general holds his army in the palm of his hand to do with it as he lists. For Tolstoi war is, above all things, the clashing of blind forces; and a great battle is a catastrophe precipitated, not by the deliberate scheming of tacticians, but by the resistless action of vast bodies of men, impelled to butcher one another by some common sentiment. How much and how little a general can direct the process of events in war may be seen from his description of the great Russian General Bagration on the field of Austerlitz :—

'He (Prince André) was very surprised to see that in reality Prince Bagration did not give any orders, and contented himself with trying to show that his general intentions were in perfect accord with what in reality was the simple result of the force of circumstances, of the will of his subordinates, and of the caprices of chance. And yet, in spite of the turn events were taking, quite outside the range of his anticipations, Prince André was obliged to admit that his tactful demeanour made his presence of the highest value. The very sight of him gave renewed self-possession to those who had approached him with agitated countenances. Officials and soldiers saluted him gaily, and vied with one another in displaying their courage in his presence.'

A thousand unexpected chances intervene between plans and their execution. Soldiers—even German soldiers—are not machines, and the battlefield is not a chess-board, and high above all the proposals of man there hovers inexorable fate, which plays in the Slav imagination of to-day almost as commanding a *rôle* as in the Greek imagination of old. And so Tolstoi does not attempt to account for that which is unaccountable; but he conveys a sense of the grandeur and the awfulness of war, and of the helplessness of the individual units engaged in it, with far greater effect than the most competent expert on military tactics could achieve. He sees it, not only in its physical aspects, but in its moral and historical significance, and the least impressionable of readers must carry away from his epic a fuller and truer conception of war than he had before. For myself, I confess that I have never been able to follow intelligently the description of a campaign in any history. For me, Tolstoi alone possesses the art of making military operations both comprehensible and attractive. And one of the reasons is his wonderful faculty for disintegrating an army, for making us realise individually the human atoms of which it is composed, instead of allowing us to regard it merely as a compact mass of human material. We see each of his characters under fire in turn—Prince André, Pierre, the two Rostov brothers—and the emotions of each are depicted with searching discernment. The courage, the *bonhomie*, the endurance of the Russian soldier are brought out in a hundred instances. Tolstoi's usual method in dealing with a campaign is to give, on the one hand, a general impression in a few broad decisive lines; and, on the other, to fill in the picture here and there with a number of detached personal experiences, sometimes trivial in themselves, but related in great detail, and invariably selected to bring out the human side of the situation. In this way the campaign of 1805, with all its complicated manœuvres, leading up to the battle of Austerlitz, which forms the central episode of the first volume, is rendered extraordinarily dramatic. We have a series of photographic views of the Emperor Alexander, of Kutusov, of Bagration; and we follow in turn the fortunes of Nicholas Rostov and Prince André on the battlefield, culminating in the meeting of Rostov with the Russian Emperor in the moment of defeat, and the interview of André with Napoleon in the hour of his triumph.

The whole of the third volume centres round the battle of Borodino and the burning of Moscow. The appalling nature of the event, and the vastness of the issues at stake, inspire the author with a passionate defence of his country. He shows us how the calamity worked in the end for good, and how it marked a turning-point in the history of the Empire. He makes us realise that the invasion of Russia by a foreign foe, and the destruction of her capital, depended on something far deeper than the personal ambition of Napoleon, or the jealousies and blundering of the Russian headquarter staff. He shows us the inevitableness of the French retreat, their helplessness in the face of Russian patriotism, which, in their work of mere aggression, they could oppose with no corresponding sentiment. He devotes many pages to the philosophy of Borodino—a battle concerning which military critics have never arrived at an agreement—and sums up the meaning of the fight in a paragraph, instinct with his wide vision of life :—

'The victory which the Russians won at Borodino . . . was one of those victories which force upon the soul of the aggressor the double conviction of the moral superiority of his adversary and of his own weakness. The French invading army was like some wild beast that had burst its chains, and had received a mortal wound in its flank ; it knew that it was hurrying to its death, but the momentum had been given, and at all risks it was bound to reach Moscow. The Russian army, on the other hand, although twice as weak, was driven inexorably into further resistance. There at Moscow, still bleeding from the wounds of Borodino, its renewed efforts resulted inevitably in the flight of Napoleon, in his retreat by the same road along which he had advanced, in the almost total loss of the 500,000 men who had followed him, and in the destruction of Napoleonic France, upon whom there had descended at Borodino the hand of an adversary, possessed of superior moral worth !'

Mingled with the fate of the Empire we have the fate of the main characters of the book. Princess Marie is driven from her home at Lissy-Gory by the invaders; and the Rostov family takes part in the flight from Moscow, which resulted in Napoleon waiting in vain at the gates of the city for the Boyars to come and do obeisance before him. Much of the campaign is related through the personal experiences of Prince André Bolkonski and Pierre Besukov. They represent the military and the civil element in the great struggle for national liberty. Prince André, a typical soldier, intelligent, self-confident, and a little hard, is wounded at Borodino ; and we have a long description of his sufferings, of his treatment in the ambulance tent, of his sensations during the retreat. But side by side with the realistic details there is the thread of his spiritual experiences, which we are never allowed to lose sight of. Pain, suffering, the near approach of death, are all appointed means of spiritual enlightenment. Bit by bit the mystery of life becomes revealed to the wounded officer, as he is jolted in his travelling carriage out of Moscow, in that hasty flight of a whole city at the approach of the invader, or as he lies at night on his camp-bed in his temporary halting-places. The infinite pettiness of this life is made plain to him; he becomes detached from all earthly interests, and a strange and radiant sense of wellbeing takes possession of his soul. His resentment against Natasha is at an end, and it is she who sits by his side and ministers to his wants while he awaits the advent of death. The luminous pages describing the last supreme struggle are as full of spiritual consciousness as an essay by Maeterlinck; the majesty of death reigns over all, so imposing that the personal grief of sister and of *fiancée* is hushed before it, and they await the inevitable in silence. Only a supreme artist could have disentangled the essential meaning of events from out of the strife and turmoil of a campaign; and from the artistic point of view, Tolstoi has written nothing more admirable than these pages.

Pierre Besukov is in all respects the opposite of his friend Prince André. In him Tolstoi has combined many of the essential characteristics of the Slav race, and he is the mouthpiece of Tolstoi's most cherished convictions on life and morals. We feel that between Pierre and the author there is on many points so complete an assimilation of ideas as to confer upon the former something of an autobiographical interest. It is through him that the great moral lessons of the book are taught. For a hero, he is a strange clumsy figure; but we realise from the first that behind his apparent timidity there lies a latent energy which in due time will take effect. He is full of faults, he is careless, selfish, addicted to drink and gambling; but in his nature there are infinite possibilities of goodness and gentleness and all-embracing charity, without which, as the author teaches us, there can be no true greatness. Pierre is a dreamer, and while pondering over the mystery of life he stumbles badly in his temporal affairs. He drifts, he hardly knows why, into a marriage with Elena Kuragine, the most beautiful woman in St. Petersburg. He does not love her, but her beauty has appealed to his lower instincts, and his will is paralysed by a sense of the fatality of life. Tolstoi describes the scenes preceding the betrothal with an almost brutal candour; we know that hundreds of marriages are made so, but no one save Tolstoi has shown the repulsive features so clearly through the gilding of conventional society. The marriage turns out a ghastly failure; Pierre fights a duel with his wife's lover; and in a moment of blind rage, to which his great physical strength renders him liable, he almost threatens to kill Elena herself. Travelling from Moscow to St. Petersburg, he is detained at a posting-house, and falls into conversation with one Basdaiev, a Freemason. Basdaiev, with unerring candour, tells Pierre some home truths; and we feel that the questions he puts to him were questions that Tolstoi must have asked of himself at a certain stage of his career, and have felt himself unable to supply the answer.

'If you look with horror on your life,'

declares Basdaiev, 'change it, purify yourself, and as fast as you succeed in reforming yourself you will learn to know wisdom. How have you spent your life? In orgies, in debauchery, in immorality, taking everything from society and giving nothing in exchange. How have you spent the fortune that you inherited? What have you done for your neighbour? Have you given a thought to your tens of thousands of serfs? Have you come to their assistance either morally or materially? No! you know you have not. You have merely profited by their labour to lead a corrupt existence. You have spent your life in idleness.'

This conversation is a first turning-point in Pierre's career. Henceforward, although in many respects he leads the same life as before, continuing to drink and gamble and frequent low company, he never again is able to stifle the inner voice of conscience. He becomes a Freemason; he practises philanthropy; he tries to ameliorate the condition of his serfs. It is of no avail. He cannot rid himself of his evil habits; and, above all, he cannot rid himself of the hideous incubus of his marriage and of the false position in which he is placed by his wife's conduct. His chivalrous love for Natasha is the one bright spot in his life of failure and disappointment. It is only when Elena dies, when the great national crisis of 1812 opens his eyes to much to which he had been blind before, and, finally, when he lives in daily intimacy with Karataiev, during the long weeks when he is dragged as a prisoner in the rear of the French army, that his spiritual conversion is definitely effected. Karataiev, even more than Pierre, is a character difficult for the Western mind to grasp. He is a typical Russian peasant, with all the simplicity and affectionate goodness and strong religious faith of his class at its best. He combines absolute stoicism under suffering with an imperturbable gaiety of mind. 'Why make yourself miserable?' he asks Pierre, as they lie side by side on the floor of the crowded prison. 'We suffer an hour, and we live a century.' His insensibility to material wants is not the insensibility which pertains to a lower order of nature; he has acquired it, because he has raised himself above that which is temporary and unessential in life. His days in prison are spent in little acts of unostentatious kindness ; his charity is all-embracing ; he does not even neglect a stray cur that has crept in among the prisoners. When he dies—shot down by the French because he is too weak to follow the retreating army—he dies in silence, with an expression of grave serenity in his eyes. Tolstoi is penetrated by a sense of the beauty of Karataiev's nature. The little peasant moves through the pages of *War and Peace* as though crowned with a halo ; and he seems to belong, not to our materialistic nineteenth century, but rather to the same plane of spiritual existence as the band of ecstatic Franciscans who gathered round the Saint of Assisi in the beautiful Umbrian plain. He personifies all that the Count holds highest and best in human nature ; and it is in keeping with the author's whole attitude towards society that this supreme example should be met with among the untaught Russian peasantry. Karataiev has all the passive virtues ; pride and self-seeking have no part in him. Pierre meets with him at a critical moment in his life, when the sufferings he had gone through, and the horrors he had witnessed, had filled his soul with despair, and had extinguished his faith in God. Contact with essential goodness is more persuasive than any sermon, and Pierre learns from Karataiev what no one else had been able to teach him. It is as a prisoner, deprived not only of the luxuries to which he was accustomed, but even of the very necessaries of life, that he acquires the peace of mind that he has sought for in vain all his life. And he finds it in the renunciation of the things of this world, in the renunciation of his own will, and in the identification of himself, his interests, his aspirations with those of the great human family around him. This is the moral teaching of *War and Peace*; but it is conveyed so eloquently in the progress of the epic, in the gradual evolution of the character of Besukov, that the author has no need to enforce it by deliberate argument. It pervades the whole story, and to it is owing a portion at least of that lofty grandeur of conception which gives to the work its unique place in literature.

If we wish to ascertain how much more than a mere picture of a campaign Tolstoi has given us, we may turn for comparison to a recent military novel, which has deservedly attracted considerable attention. I refer to *Le Désastre* by the brothers Margueritte. It gives the history of the Franco-German war up to the fall of Metz, interwoven with a slight thread of romance, and it is written throughout in a tone of moderation, almost of *bonhomie*, which one would not have expected to find under the circumstances in a French author. Some of the descriptions, that of the Emperor quitting the army, and the cavalry charge at Gravelottes, are admirable pieces of writing ; and we have a gruesome, yet not overladen, picture of the delays, the blunders, the incapacity which led to the final capitulation of the French army. The authors have had to contend with the exceptional difficulty of investing with a romantic interest an uninterrupted series of military disasters, disgraceful alike to the army and the nation, and to have built up so readable a narrative from such depressing material is proof of no slight literary dexterity. Yet something indefinable is missing, something that throws the halo of poetry over the scenes in *War and Peace*, something that constitutes the irresistible charm of Tolstoi's book. The very obvious merits of *Le Désastre* only serve to render the charm between it and *War and Peace* the more marked : it is the immeasurable difference between a work of genius and one of painstaking merit.

But the book before us is not all war and moral philosophy; it has its lighter, almost its frivolous side. Tolstoi's wide outlook on life does not blind him to the details of domestic life, to the characteristic futilities of social intercourse. Not Jane Austen herself chronicles the small talk of her characters with greater zest and accuracy than the seer of Yasnaia Poliana. Even so banal a subject as a girl's first ball he invests with a delightfully fresh aspect. The doings and sayings of quite young people possess a special charm for him; his sympathy with their aspirations is complete and intuitive; and his description of the schoolroom party in the Rostov mansion, their quarrels and flirtations and innocent escapades, while written with no apparent motive save that of the *raconteur*, serve as a valuable basis for his masterly studies of character. He has a wonderful faculty, a supreme gift in a novelist, of winning our sympathies for his characters almost with a word. His few touches describing Lisa Bolkonski, the 'little princess' at Anna Pavlovna's evening party, her gay smile, her childish manner, her bewitching upper lip, with the slight down upon it, endear her to us straightway. He paints her with all the tenderness of one who knows that a great tragedy is to befall her. Lisa in reality is an uninteresting, frivolous little person, and Tolstoi is quite conscious of the fact; yet when she dies in childbirth with a scared interrogative expression on her upturned face, as though she were asking of one and all, 'What have you done to me?' we understand, better perhaps than we understood before, the capacity for suffering that is inherent in even the most trivial human soul. Another quite subsidiary character, who yet is endowed with an extraordinary charm, is Petia, the youngest member of the Rostov family. He is simply a high-spirited schoolboy, who at sixteen, in the terrible year of the taking of Moscow, persuades his reluctant parents to allow him to enlist. Nothing in all the long battle scenes brings home the horror of war more piercingly than the little episode of the boy-soldier losing his head in the excitement of his first skirmish, and galloping wildly to his death. And his mother's tears—though a mother's grief at the loss of a son is the very commonplace of war—affect us like some personal sorrow.

It is Tolstoi's intense humanity, his capacity for putting himself in the place of each of his characters in turn, for seeing life from their point of view, that gives to them their appealing charm. They are so real, so like ourselves, that we can enter into all their feelings, all their follies and temptations. Of no one is this more true than of Natasha, the most delightful of heroines. We love her from the moment of her first appearance on the stage, Natasha at thirteen, in a short muslin frock, tearing into her mother's drawing-room with a doll in her arms; or, again, at the big family banquet, raising her shrill little voice to ask her mother down the long table, 'Mamma, what pudding will there be?' And yet Natasha is far from a model young lady. She flirts openly with Denissov and her music-master; she is engaged first to Boris Droubetzkoi, her playmate, then to Prince André; and in the absence of the latter during the period of betrothal, she attempts to elope with the worthless Anatole Kuragine in a wild fit of uncontrollable passion. She nurses Prince André when he is wounded with an absorbed devotion, and mourns him sincerely; yet but a few weeks later, urged on by the irresistible needs of her nature, she is giving definite encouragement to Pierre Besukov. It is her intense naturalness, her virginal candour, which save her from all blame. There is a straightforward simplicity about the Russian character which is not to be met with in our more sophisticated Western States. Russians are far closer to primitive society than we; they have scarcely more than a century of civilisation behind them. Natasha is an impulsive child, and she follows the dictates of her untamed girlish nature, of her buoyant animal spirits. Love is a necessity to her; as a child she adored Sonia, her mother, her brothers, and demanded constant proofs of their affection. Her love for Prince André is genuine, but she cannot endure his cold self-restraint, his apparent indifference to her feelings; she frets and fumes at his absence; and in a moment of hysterical craving she is ready to give herself to the handsome Anatole, who has appealed to all her lower instincts. The sufferings and the tragedy of 1812 leave their mark on her, as on every one, and it is a tamed and subdued Natasha who marries Pierre in the end. But even in marriage she is very far from imitating the conventional type of the perfect wife. She is frankly jealous and *exigeante*, and we learn that she neglected all those outward charms and accomplishments by which the prudent spouse is supposed to hold her husband in bondage. In this, however, she seems to act in accordance with the Count's own views of wifely conduct. For we are told with some asperity that it would have appeared as ridiculous to her husband as to herself had she worried him with her elegant pretensions, and that their happiness rested on something far more solid than the poetic charm that first attracted Besukov to her.

How far Natasha fulfils Tolstoi's ideal of womanhood I cannot say; but it is clear from the way in which his pen lingers round her, chronicling her most fugitive thoughts and actions, that he entertains for her to the full that indulgent affection that he has known how to excite on her behalf in all his readers. It is in a quite different spirit that he describes the Princess Marie Bolkonski, the sister of Prince André. She is drawn with a tender reverence, for his model was his own mother. But even Princess Marie is not idealised. We are told that she had a wooden figure and walked on her heels; we are shown her plain face with her hair drawn back from her forehead and her blotchy complexion; but her innate purity and goodness transpires through it all, and her beautiful smile makes up for every deficiency. Even in the scene when Prince Basil comes to ask her hand in marriage for his son Anatole—for Princess Marie is an heiress, and Anatole has run through his father's fortune—and her sister-in-law dresses her up to receive her prospective lover, and renders her plainer than ever, her refined distinction of soul carries her with dignity through the ordeal.

The picture of life at Lissy-Gory in its appalling monotony, the old Prince tyrannising alike over daughter and dependants, and scaring away possible visitors by the inflexible rigidity of his demeanour, is as characteristically true of one aspect of Russian provincial life in the past as the gay and reckless hospitality of the Rostov family at Otradnoë is true of another. Through Princess Marie the reader is brought in touch with one of the most curious developments of Russian religious life, the poor pilgrims whose days are spent wandering from shrine to shrine, supported by the arms of the faithful. Many of them are little better than idle beggars, yet among them is to be found much of the vague but sincere religious sentiment which in England finds an outlet in the dissenting bodies, but which in Russia can find no free expression save within the recognised boundaries of the Orthodox Church. Princess Marie herself, a model of humility and goodness, deeply reverenced her humble friends;

she even kept a pilgrim's robe hidden away in her cupboard, hoping some day to don it and to share at once in their material privations and their spiritual ecstasies. The scene when André and Pierre come upon the Princess giving tea to two representatives of 'God's people' in her sitting-room is so intensely Slav in sentiment, that for us of Western Europe it is like peeping into another world. We know that it is painted from life, for Count Tolstoi surrounds himself with these humble pilgrims in his home in the country. And if he does not always approve of the forms in which religious zeal clothes itself in Russia, he is in the fullest sympathy with the spirit that inspires them, and he writes of them with an unquestioning reverence.

There is no need for Tolstoi to award praise or blame to his characters; he never explains when they should be deserving of either; they speak for themselves. His sinners are as human as his saints; and there is not one for whom, almost unconsciously, he does not enlist some measure of our sympathy. Often his silence will enlighten as much as the speech of another.

Of Elena he paints nothing save the beautiful exterior; we understand, without being told, that her nature is rotten to the core, that there is no soul to illuminate the exquisitely chiselled mask of her face. Even to Dologhor and Anatole he allows a few elementary virtues; his sense of the universal frailty of mankind is too keen for him to indulge in harsh judgments. He sees with unerring perception the double nature that is in each one of us. Nothing is more masterly in its very slightness than his analysis of the character of Prince Basil, the father of Anatole and Elena. The ordinary novelist would have shown him merely as a worldly intriguer; but somehow Tolstoi makes us feel that there was in him some subtle personal element which gave him distinction, and we are almost ready to forgive him his unscrupulous scheming. Yet we know that in his three worthless children he has the punishment he deserves.

That the author of two such books as *War and Peace* and *Anna Karenina* should have relinquished novel-writing for any other work, however engrossing and important, cannot but be a matter of regret for all lovers of romantic literature. It is a sacrifice on the altar of duty with which in this instance it is difficult to feel in sympathy; for Count Tolstoi takes his place among the very greatest of novelists. He may not possess the delicate pellucid charm of a Turgenev, or the descriptive power of a Flaubert; he may not be a stylist like Théophile Gautier, but none the less he is a giant in the world of romance, such another giant as Victor Hugo. Though in many respects they stand poles asunder, both Hugo and Tolstoi are endowed with a patriarchal greatness which places them in a class apart in their respective countries. And *Les Misérables* has always seemed to me the one and only novel which in imaginative power and vastness of conception can claim to be judged by the same standard as *War and Peace*. It also is rather an epic than a romance. Each is the fruit of a mighty brain, compared with which the many clever little writers of to-day seem puny indeed. By his literary work Count Tolstoi belongs, together with Turgenev and Gogol and Dostoievski, to that middle of the century which in Russia, as in France, was a golden age in romantic literature. His friends and contemporaries are dead, but the Count still lives, a venerable bearded figure in the garb of a moujik boldly preaching an interpretation of Christianity carried to a logical conclusion from which men in all ages have shrunk. He has put behind him the writing of romances as unworthy dilettantism, as a dangerous tampering with the evil things in our social system. And yet—so different are the ultimate judgments of posterity from our own, and from those of our contemporaries—it may well be as the author of *Anna Karenina*, and the writer of the greatest prose epic of his century, that the would-be social reformer will receive the permanent homage of mankind.